PRAISE FOR

TREASURE HUNT & MICHAEL HINKLE

"I value the past two decades of working with you as GHA communities sales account manager for the First American Title Company; as in most businesses, a core principle and what is said of business professionals it's who they surround themselves with that is a direct reflection of their success, building strong viable relationships and creating a strong team …. a team leader that you can rely on under any circumstance, as has been my experience working with you and my new home building company. Communication is the key to success, and you have mastered this.

It's not what happens to you in your life that determines the outcome, it's what you do about what happens. This concept comes to mind when thinking of our past business relationship, as it exemplifies your positive attitude toward life, business, and, more importantly, people. This philosophy that is a reflection of your culture has contributed to the success of GHA, and I know for many, many other of your clients, and has led you to have a commitment to your customers that shows itself in attention to detail and follow through, of high-level customer service, and persistence to close the transaction with the client's goal in mind, putting your customers first is so honorable and not commonly understood by many.

It has been a genuine pleasure to work with you, your passion, commitment of your time and your personal and professional levels over the past two decades that I have come to rely on. Your innate abilities have been unparalleled to myself and staff, an important part of our business team that will be missed. It is nice to know that you are committed to sharing your years of experience with others; there is nothing better than sharing this passion, for others to have the tools and direction to succeed. Thank you and good luck my friend for you and your willingness to always go the extra mile."

MARIO J. GONZALES
CEO AND PRESIDENT, GHA COMMUNITIES

"What Michael has brought to our business over the years can be put into many categories including excellent service, extensive knowledge of his field, the ability to navigate his corporate environment to benefit his clients, and the willingness to go to bat for us in difficult situations. Those traits are why we have continued our relationship to this day. They are not, however, why we initially gave Michael our business that then led to more than a decade of us working together.

Michael was persistent. He called on our company for years before getting any business, showing up at the office at least once per month to say hi, drop off collateral, and ask if we needed anything. We never did. We had perfectly good relationships with other companies and their reps, and we were not looking forward to making a change.

That is until one day those relationships had soured, and we had a need. By that time, we had gotten to know Michael. He was knowledgeable, worked for a reputable company and never gave us a hard sell, just asking if he could help us with anything. It was not a difficult decision to make the call to bring him in and sit down to talk about the next steps.

Those next steps were, in hindsight, an extension of Mike's sales philosophy. All the hard work put in over the ensuing years putting deals together and working through challenges and obstacles was Michael continuing to sell us his services. Not selling the services of his Fortune 500 employer, but on HIS services and how he could benefit our company. His services continue to benefit our company today."

DAVE BARISIC
PRINCIPAL, BRANDYWINE HOMES

TREASURE HUNT

MICHAEL HINKLE

TREASURE HUNT

A COMMON-SENSE APPROACH
TO BUILDING A SUCCESSFUL SALES CAREER

Advantage | Books

Published by Advantage Books, Charleston, South Carolina.
An imprint of Advantage Media.

ADVANTAGE is a registered trademark, and the Advantage colophon is a trademark of Advantage Media Group, Inc.

Printed in the United States of America.

10 9 8 7 6 5 4 3 2 1

ISBN: 978-1-64225-739-7 (Paperback)
ISBN: 978-1-64225-738-0 (eBook)

Library of Congress Control Number: 2023916741

Book design by Matthew Morse.

This publication is designed to provide accurate and authoritative information in regard to the subject matter covered. It is sold with the understanding that the publisher is not engaged in rendering legal, accounting, or other professional services. If legal advice or other expert assistance is required, the services of a competent professional person should be sought.

Advantage Books is an imprint of Advantage Media Group. Advantage Media helps busy entrepreneurs, CEOs, and leaders write and publish a book to grow their business and become the authority in their field. Advantage authors comprise an exclusive community of industry professionals, idea-makers, and thought leaders. For more information go to **advantagemedia.com**.

Vicki, my bride of 33+ years and the one person who has supported me through so much of the journey that made this book possible. To Matthew, Bryan, and Candice, my children who gave me a reason every day to suit up and show up to provide my family with everything they needed.

CONTENTS

ACKNOWLEDGMENTS

A special thank you to Victoria Tabb, my life coach for the last seven years and the person who challenged and then inspired me to author this book. Without her pushing and assistance, all the life stories as well as the lessons learned over my career would never have come to light.

INTRODUCTION

A long time ago, someone shared with me the best kept secret in sales:

SALES IS A TREASURE HUNT.

"Imagine you're standing at the edge of a massive field," they said. "And that field is littered with thousands of rocks of all shapes and sizes. Now, imagine a few of those rocks are hiding something of great value. Some have a huge chunk of gold underneath; others may have smaller pieces of gold or silver. But a large percentage of rocks have absolutely *nothing* underneath them at all. What would you do?"

Most people would say they'd develop a systematic approach to search under every single rock until they have found everything of value. Seems like common sense, right?

And yet, that's not what ends up happening in reality.

Some treasure hunters start out hyped up. They might target a few massive boulders assuming there must be large pieces of gold underneath. But when the initial results disappoint them, they give up. Maybe they think they were misled, feeling bitter and discouraged as they abandon the search.

Others may dawdle at the edge of the field and look under a few rocks, at first attempting to use a system, but then they get bored with it and jump over to another system. And then another. And then, gradually, there's no more system whatsoever, it's just happenstance, picking up whatever rock draws their attention in the moment. They might get lucky a few times and find a few coins along the way but eventually, they become jaded and leave the field completely. They know the treasure is there—they just don't have the endurance to keep searching.

The above-average treasure hunter, though, will set a course of action to turn over every rock in the field. They will literally leave "no stone unturned." They won't get discouraged by the many stones with nothing underneath; instead, they'll adopt the positive attitude, "This just means I'm one stone closer to finding a piece of treasure." Maybe they even find some rocks with treasure underneath, but it's frozen in the ground—it's the wrong time to collect. So they continue moving, but with a plan to come back when the ground has thawed.

Finding success in sales is really no different from becoming this third type of treasure hunter. Ever since this image was shared with me, it's become the model for what I've done my entire sales career. And guess what? It's served me really well.

It's been my experience that not many people dream of becoming a sales professional—and I'm no exception. My first job was in public service, working for Riverside County in my home state of California as a real estate property agent. After several years sitting across from salespeople being pitched to, I realized I wanted to be the one *delivering* the pitch. With sales, I saw an avenue to give myself a raise without having to wait for others to decide what I was worth.

I'll share more about my journey in the first chapter, but for now, it's enough for you to know I've worked in sales in various markets, run my own company, learned new skills, and experienced setbacks in both my personal and professional life. All of this has helped me learn how to be a better treasure hunter.

But I've discovered that what I define as treasure has changed over time. My view of success has shifted from the monetary rewards of sales to helping others achieve the success they want. It's my new Why—helping others become treasure hunters, too.

CHANGING THE LANDSCAPE

It's past time to change the landscape in how sales is viewed. Despite all the new tools which promise larger and easier sales—from cloud-based CRMs, to social media strategies, to outsourced lead generation—the average sales rep turnover rate is a staggering 35 percent … nearly three times higher than all other industries.[1] But why?

For starters, let's state the obvious: sales is *hard*.

Being in sales means signing up to be told "no" over and over, facing rejection, and volunteering to be on the frontline of a client's rage when something goes wrong. This can wear anyone down. I like to think I have pretty thick skin, but after three decades of experi-

FOR STARTERS, LET'S STATE THE OBVIOUS: SALES IS *HARD*.

ence, there are still days where even I get discouraged.

For the purpose of our discussion, though, the root for "sales burnout" is twofold:

- First, it's a mindset problem. Sales professionals often approach their work with a completely wrong mindset. They're focused

---

1   Rachel Cravat, "Sales turnover: Why doing less costs more [+ calculator]," Spiff.com, April 21, 2022, accessed March 6, 2023, https://spiff.com/blog/sales-turnover-cost-calculator/.

on transactions when they should be focused on building relationships. Transactions are fleeting; the joy from them dissipates as quickly as it comes. Relationships last longer, are stronger, and produce more impact and reward.

- Second, it's a tactical problem. Sales professionals are overdependent on tools and underdependent on skills. There's nothing wrong with having tools like a CRM or a lead generator, but with the right skills, the specific tools don't matter so much. Great skills transfer over to nearly any tool you want to use—and augment the effectiveness of those tools.

I've seen this to be true because my thirty years as a sales professional have seen a lot of change in the industry, especially with the advent of the internet and cloud-based technology. What haven't changed a bit for me are the fundamental skills of sales, which I have seen time and again with my own mindset and tactical problems.

In this book, I want to tackle both of these problems side-by-side because they can't be separated. Our mindset drives our tactics, that is, our actions. And our actions must be empowered by the right mindset.

Whether you're just starting out in sales or you're a tenured sales pro in charge of a sales team, it's high time we reframe the sales conversation. Success in sales is fundamentally about how effectively you communicate with people—period. And successful communication requires both the right mindset and right skills working in tandem.

A lot of what you'll find here isn't too revolutionary—it's almost all common sense. We humans just get easily distracted (especially this human here), and we don't always see common sense at first. Most of what we discuss should be minor shifts for you. If you can make those minor shifts, they will have a major impact on your experience as a sales professional.

NO STONE UNTURNED

A few years ago, I was in a state of transition. I was adapting to life as an empty-nester while feeling like my career had plateaued. I found myself reevaluating a lot of what was happening in my life—what was important to me and where to go from there. Something I discovered in this process was my desire to have a life coach to help me gain some perspective.

In our conversations, we analyzed where my career had come from by looking at my past and talking through how my mind processes decisions, especially in the context of sales. Unlike other career plateaus, mine wasn't so much about getting stuck—it was more about not knowing what else I wanted to achieve.

As we dived into this, I shared with her what had made me successful and some of my frustrations about the current world of sales. She felt like I had a unique way of looking at the industry and encouraged me to start jotting down my thoughts.

Following her advice, I noticed some themes in what I was writing down. I saw a pattern of how my approach to clients was different from my peers. I began to see how my take on sales had consistently set me up for success. It wasn't luck at all—it was how I viewed sales and, specifically, my relationship to prospects.

Speaking of coaching, I got my first taste of being a coach when I was eighteen and just starting my life as an adult. I was part of a swim club and fell in love with coaching others and helping them get better at swimming.

This love for coaching opened the way for me to move past the career plateau I was going through. In 2012, I started up JBI (Just Buy In), so I could coach others in sales and pass on all I've learned. While I don't expect the people I coach to do *everything* exactly the way I do, my philosophy is that if a strategy helps me, then maybe you can find a golden nugget to help you achieve the success you want.

With JBI, my job is to share these insights with the next generation of salespeople. The techniques and strategies I've used to be successful are not unique to me—they're all teachable for those who are coachable. Everything I teach my JBI clients are in these pages—the principles and practices became the acorn for this book.

By reevaluating my own goals, I've found a new sense of purpose—to share my framework to help others reframe their view of sales and replicate the success I've enjoyed. After all, the analogy I shared about the field and hidden treasure wasn't my own original thought—it was shared with me. That one idea completely altered my view of sales in the best ways and set me up for success. And now it's my turn to do the same thing for others.

That said, my mission for the remainder of this book is to help you reframe sales—to shift from seeing it as a job you do to seeing it as a business you own. To move away from mediocre short-term strategies to long-term thinking, which actually produces results. To move from depending on chance to creating opportunities.

Sales is a treasure hunt. Time to go hunting.

CHAPTER 1

THE FARMER AND THE HUNTER

The outdoors has always felt like a second home. Growing up in Northern California, I spent as much time as possible outside. I was in Boy Scouts my entire childhood, so you could find me hunting for rocks and natural minerals, camping—but *never* standing still. I always had to be on the move, seeking adventure.

Hunting is a way of life where I grew up—deer and dove, to be specific. Since my dad was a disabled vet who'd lost his leg in an accident, he wasn't able to take me out hunting himself. Instead, he had several friends who would take me out hunting with them so I wouldn't miss out on the experience.

I still remember my first time hunting when my dad's friend came to pick me up in his Jeep. We spent a lot of time working ridge lines, searching the terrain for any evidence of deer. We were *constantly* moving.

As we walked, my dad's friend taught me the signs to look for—how to recognize the types of groves and areas where deer normally bedded down, looking for water sources, spotting isolated stands in the forest with a clearing around them, boxed-in canyons, or hilltops. He taught me to first look for a doe, because "Wherever there's a doe, there's going to be bucks."

Later on, I learned it was the same when you bird hunt. You're out there walking, looking to flush birds out, eyes on the ground. When a dove takes off, you point the open end of your gun in his general direction, pull the trigger, and hopefully you're a good shot. Otherwise, you're a vegetarian, I suppose.

Being on the move is the only kind of hunting I've ever known. I've never hunted from a deer stand or any other stationary position. I'm a patient guy, but I don't think I'd have the patience that style of hunting requires. Even when I'm sitting, I probably drive people batty because my leg's always bouncing a hundred miles an hour.

The essential concept here is *movement*. Hunters are always on the move because their prey is on the move, too. Likewise, sales is not a static environment. It's constantly in motion.

With more than thirty years in sales, I've seen a lot of changes in the industry. From the days of the rolodex and landline phone to the advent of social media and cloud-based sales management platforms. But one thing hasn't changed: the most successful salespeople are those who create—or hunt—their own opportunities.

EVERYONE IS IN SALES

I spend a lot of my time helping people reframe their view of sales, making a shift in how they view the profession. When I talk with many other sales professionals, whether it's through my sales coaching at JBI or a speaking engagement, the gist is the same. They see sales as a job, not as a career. There are a few problems with this thinking.

For starters, I'm a firm believer that *everyone* is in sales, whether you have "sales" in your job title or not. In both our personal and professional lives, we live in a world where we are constantly *selling* someone on an idea. If you apply for a mortgage, you're selling the lender on the state of your finances and the idea that you deserve the home loan. If you're at your annual physical, you're selling your doctor on your lifestyle choices. If you're asking someone out on a date, you're having to sell yourself as someone they will enjoy spending time with.

Zig Ziglar once expressed this same belief when he said, "If the business you are in requires you to deal with people, you, my friend, are in sales."[2]

What I particularly love about this quote is how he connects the idea of *business* with *people*. I'd be lying to say I haven't had

> **SALES IS JUST THE SWITCH YOU FLIP TO TRANSFORM A PROBLEM FROM *UNSOLVED* TO *SOLVED*.**

help from others in my long career. The heart of a successful business is rooted in people helping one another solve problems. Sales is just the switch you flip to transform a problem from *unsolved* to *solved*.

I've always loved helping people solve problems, which is why I initially entered public service. At my first "real" job, I worked for Riverside County in California. Most of my time there was spent as a real estate property agent—leasing out county land for various activities, such as equestrian, recreational, and agricultural uses—in addition to leasing office and warehouse spaces. If someone needed space from the county, I was the one helping negotiate the terms.

---

2   Zig Ziglar, BrainyQuote.com, accessed March 6, 2023, https://www.brainyquote.com/quotes/zig_ziglar_617802.

I was young, and after a few years, I ran into a situation where I was told I'd need another six years or so before I could be seriously considered for promotion. In all of my negotiations at this point, I'd spent a ton of time sitting across from salespeople, learning what they did, learning how they earned their commissions. Suddenly, I realized, "Hey, I want to be on the other side of the table here. I want to be the one doing the selling."

Given the real estate knowledge I'd gained, I felt the easiest place to start out was as a commercial industrial real estate broker where I was commission-only. This only lasted a year—partly because I was also going through a divorce. There's never a good time for that, of course, but this one was particularly ill-timed.

When the smoke cleared, I jumped over to work for a mortgage company, which is when my career really took off. My personal life turned around too as I met my wife Vicki and remarried. By my second year, I was number three in the company and moved into a sales management position.

A quick word on sales management, though—too many successful salespeople move into management and then toss the sales book out the window. They think they no longer need to use their skills. Probably the smartest move I ever made as a sales manager was to eschew this way of thinking. Instead, I told myself, "If I want to be good at managing salespeople, then I better keep being good at sales myself." So I kept on selling.

I saw plenty of ups and downs in the mortgage market, and eventually started up my own company selling residential real estate. In this process, I also started up an independent company for notarization. Not many others were doing this at the time—notarization wasn't seen as a big deal. But this allowed me to carve out a niche for myself, catering to escrow and title companies who were closing on new construction properties.

Eventually, I was approached by a key executive my wife worked for. He was making a move over to a large, national title company and wanted us to come along. We took him up on the offer, spent a few years there, and in time, we all joined another Fortune 500 title company where I have happily spent the past twenty-plus years.

One of the inspirations for this book was my belief there are not enough people still practicing the art

WHAT IF SALES COULD BECOME KNOWN LESS FOR THE TRANSACTION AND MORE FOR PROBLEM-SOLVING?

of creating a business from scratch. Since businesses are built on sales, *sales* shouldn't be a dirty word. Once you accept the concept of everyone being in the business of sales, you can see the role of salesperson as the necessary position it is.

REFRAMING SALES AS A BUSINESS

The second problem with viewing sales only as an employment position involves the most important mental shift we'll return to throughout this book: the idea of viewing your sales career the same as building a business.

Sales has gotten a bad reputation as the result of bad sales strategies—and bad salespeople. Even if you are a sales professional yourself, you've probably also been guilty of "putting up a wall" when approached by another salesperson. Why? Because no one wants to be talked into or feel forced into a decision—especially when it involves money.

But what if sales could earn a new reputation? What if sales could become known less for the transaction and more for problem-solving?

When I discuss sales with younger professionals, I encourage them to enter the field with the mind of a business owner—and to control every aspect of their career the same way a business owner would. Oftentimes, they overlook the big picture of sales. They don't see their role is to generate revenue for the whole company, which is then used to pay all the employees. This is an ownership mentality.

> **EVERY BUSINESS NEEDS SALES TO EXIST. BUSINESSES THAT FAIL TO BE SALES-DRIVEN DON'T GET TO STAY IN BUSINESS FOR LONG.**

Instead, sales professionals often only look at how much of the sale they get to keep, which leads to feeling underappreciated. But this is the mindset of someone who sees sales as a job and not as a career. If your focus is only on what you get for yourself, with no thought to the overall well-being of the organization, then you're only seeing sales through the lens of an employee.

I see this commission-centered thinking come up a lot in my coaching clients at JBI. And to be frank, it was my thinking too when I was first starting out. Now, I don't believe there's any such thing as a purely altruistic individual. We all have to take care of ourselves and our families. But when you reframe sales as a business, it means you're also focused on the success of the company, because that's how an owner thinks. But the sales you generate don't terminate with you. They are helping feed the families of everyone in the company. That's how important you are!

Let's acknowledge a fact: Every business needs sales to exist. Businesses that fail to be sales-driven don't get to stay in business for long. Every successful entrepreneur knows this, and better yet, they understand there won't be any sales without solving a problem.

To solve a problem, you have to first *understand* the problem. To understand the problem, you have to first get to know the prospect.

While most sales professionals implicitly understand these ideas and even teach them, somewhere along the line, the sales conversation consistently becomes more about hitting a number than about problem-solving. Seeing your sales career through the eyes of an entrepreneur is the pivot point.

I like to think of it this way: I operate as a sales rep like I'm running my own company. Even though I'm selling someone else's product or service, my focus is on selling my reputation, building my brand. These aren't conflicts.

You want to know the only true difference between a business owner and a sales representative? The business owner has to pay to create the product/service, pay for overhead, and sell the product/service.

Meanwhile, the sales rep has little to no startup costs involved. In fact, you're getting paid to build your business by selling someone else's product—a product you don't have to create! But otherwise, the sales rep mindset should be an *entrepreneurial* mindset.

I've been fortunate to work for organizations that saw greater value in encouraging me to create my own opportunities rather than providing me with limited sales leads. Sales isn't really so different from the rest of life—the biggest rewards go to the individuals who can create their own opportunities. If you look company to company, without exception, you'll see this same story play out—the most successful salespeople hunt for their own treasure.

How do they do this? By solving problems.

Consider this: Would you take your car to a mechanic who asks *you* how to fix your car? Or would you take your car to the mechanic who asks you for the car's symptoms—and then provides a plan for fixing the problem?

The answer's obvious, of course. I suggest we all take the same approach in our sales careers. There are plenty of problems in this world, but the best-paid people—the best businesspeople—are those who can identify the problem and create a valuable solution.

The world is filled with people, which means it's filled with problems. Salespeople play an essential role in solving those problems. While there're many different types of people in the world, I'm a firm believer there're only two types of salespeople: Farmers and Hunters.

THE SALES FARMER

Sales Farmers are salespeople who get introduced to a client already doing business with the company. Their role is to service an existing account with the responsibility to "tend the soil and take care of the crop," if you will. They don't venture off to find new deals.

This is the predominant version of sales I see today. Most salespeople want leads provided for them. There's nothing inherently wrong with this—there's definitely a place for Sales Farmers, especially for companies that have a continuous influx of inquiries which need to be addressed in a timely manner.

In the same way an agricultural farmer can generally predict their crop output based on the weather and seasons, a Sales Farmer can more or less predict how many accounts they can close within a specific sales season.

So don't take this as me bashing Sales Farmers at all. They play an important role in the market by helping solve problems! I've known lots of good Sales Farmers with successful careers, and some have made very good money. It's just never been my cup of tea. Frankly, I don't have the specific brand of patience it requires because I don't like waiting for prospects to come to me. For those who do, there's an appealing consistency to being a Sales Farmer.

THE SALES HUNTER

Yet I've found the salespeople I've admired the most weren't Farmers at all … they were Sales Hunters. These are the salespeople who go out and *look* for new clients. They seek out people who can possibly benefit from their product or service. They identify the client's problems, figure out how the two could integrate into a partnership, and then develop a campaign to bring the client on board.

It's a mindset built on long-term reward through building a relationship, not just conducting a transaction.

Sales Hunters combine two key qualities: patience *and* tenacity. It's critical these two go hand-in-hand.

In the introduction, I shared the picture of being in front of a parcel of vacant land strewn with rocks—some have treasure beneath them, but most don't. Patience combined with tenacity means you don't get discouraged or dissuaded from searching the entire field just because the first few rocks have nothing underneath them. You systematically move through the entire field, turning over every rock until you find every scrap of buried treasure.

Maybe some rocks don't have gold under them, but they might have a bit of wisdom, market advice, clues which can get you one step closer to finding the next piece of gold. The point is to keep moving rock to rock because there's millions of dollars beneath some of them.

As I already mentioned, Sales Farmers have patience, too—but there's less tenacity to their strategy. Their style of patience is rooted in the ability to *wait*. The brand of patience for Sales Hunters differs because they're always on the move, looking for signs of business and moving toward the opportunity. This brand of patience is more about *endurance*.

You'll typically see this sales strategy referred to as "cold calling," but let me be clear here: we're not talking about cold calling where you sit in a cubicle mindlessly "dialing for dollars." That's more like fishing—endlessly casting your line until you catch something. You've probably even heard "cold calling" compared to fishing. The thinking here is "The more times you cast out your line, the more fish you catch." But hunting is *not* fishing.

Sales Hunting means creating a client where no client previously existed. Going out into the community and creating business opportunities where none existed before. It's about knowing the signs to look for, building relationships, and solving problems as they arise. You tell me—what's cold about that?

In the next chapter, we'll get into some more of the details for what makes a successful Hunter in sales. But first, you need to understand there're two types of Sales Hunters: Established Hunters and Startup Hunters.

ESTABLISHED HUNTERS

Personally, I've always been an Established Hunter. This is where my prospects already know the company and product I have to offer. For instance, if I sell Xerox machines, I'm not having to educate anyone on what it can do for them—they already know the value of a printer/

copier and the problems it solves. Proof of being "established" is when your company name turns into a verb: "Can you Xerox this for me?"

You could see a similar analogy in comparing Coke and Pepsi. Both are soft drinks, but Coca-Cola was already a firmly established brand when Pepsi emerged on the market in 1965. With their nearly seventy-year head start, a Coke salesman in 1966 could walk into any business and everyone knew who he represented; all he had to ask was "How much do you need?" A Pepsi salesman, on the other hand, would have to first explain what Pepsi was before even getting into their sales pitch, not to mention fighting the battle of objections like, "Yes, but we already know we like Coke."

For Established Hunters, the focus tends to be on *why* your solution is the best for the prospect's specific set of problems since there is already a reputation preceding you. You'll still run into challenges, especially when there's more than one established name in your field, or the prospects who say, "I tried Coke once and didn't like it," but at least you're not having to educate them on who you are.

THE STARTUP HUNTER

Being a Startup Hunter means no one knows who you are or what you do. At least, not yet. The challenge here is unique because there's a lot of education that has to happen on the front end. You may even have to do a lot of work into revealing a problem the prospect doesn't even realize they have. After this initial hurdle, you still have to also convince them your solution is the right one for the problem.

Going back to our Pepsi example from above, there is plenty of hope for the Startup Hunter to become an Established Hunter. Everyone knows who Pepsi is now. The point being that every established business out there was once a startup, so even Established

Hunters like myself have a lot they can learn from entrepreneurial-minded Startup Hunters.

Most professional salespeople are in the category of Established Hunters, so most of our conversation will focus there. Still, the entrepreneurial business-building mindset of the Startup Hunter is key for Established Hunters to adopt. Time and again, I've seen how successful Sales Hunters incorporate a Startup Hunter mentality with great results.

In fact, I want to tell you about one of my first JBI clients. He's a young man in his mid-twenties who came to me because he had just recently started his first sales-driven role in his career. Discovering just how hard sales can be, he hired me to help him out.

Early on, I presented him with the opportunity to focus on being a Sales Farmer or Sales Hunter. I'd help him with whatever he felt was best, but I admit I was excited when he chose Hunter. After three months of working together, by making a mindset shift and practicing the strategies in this book, he saw his production double. I can't wait to see where he is three years from now!

THE BUSINESS OF SALES

When my life coach encouraged me to start writing these ideas down, I came to realize how much of successful sales strategy aligns with successful business building. Even when you're an Established Hunter working for a company and selling their product, if you can switch your thinking from "sell a product" to "build a business," it makes a world of difference in how you approach opportunities.

For one thing, entrepreneurs think about the long term. Consider some of the wealthiest people in the world—Jeff Bezos, Bill Gates, Warren Buffet—none of them inherited their wealth. They all built it. The most successful entrepreneurs in the world didn't get there because of a "get rich quick scheme." It was because they developed and executed a long-term strategy, building relationships and a reputation.

In other words, not every rock they turned over had gold underneath. But they kept turning over rocks. Patience and tenacity.

When you can view your sales career as a business to build, it refocuses your attention to productivity with a purpose. One of the biggest problems I see in current sales strategy is salespeople filling up their time with busy activities, getting lost in the minutia of helping clients with technical problems—but isn't this why we have customer service staff? There are other ways you can be customer-focused which will produce a new sale *and* better serve the customer you already have.

ACTIVITY FOR ACTIVITY'S SAKE? NOT A GOOD STRATEGY. ACTIVITY WITH A PURPOSE? VERY GOOD STRATEGY.

Another issue I see is when salespeople spend hours on low-reward activities with no potential gain when their time, energy, and actions should be invested toward achieving the goal. What's the goal? Find a new client, bring the new client on board, and make money through properly servicing them.

Activity for activity's sake? Not a good strategy.

Activity with a purpose? Very good strategy.

Which goes back to what I learned about hunting deer as a kid. When we headed out, we knew our purpose—track down a buck and bring it down. Knowing our purpose, we made sure we had the right equipment. If you're going after a buck, you don't take a slingshot or a handgun. You take a rifle!

Successful hunters go out appropriately equipped. It does you no good to know the signs if you don't have the resources available to help you execute. The resources you take along should demonstrate you have a clear picture of what prey you are after.

The same thing's true in Sales Hunting as you track down clients. These are the two most important qualifiers successful Sales Hunters use to make sure they're hitting the right target:

"Do they need my services?" Put another way: "Can I help them solve a problem?"

"Is there enough volume to justify my efforts?" That is, "Is the potential reward worth the effort?"

On this first question, what good is it to track someone who has no need for your service? All you'll do is waste time—yours and theirs. A lot of this boils down to knowing where your prospects can be found. If you're hunting deer, you don't go wandering off into elk country.

On the second question, if a hunter needs to bring home venison to feed a large family, then why waste bullets on shooting the rabbits crossing your path? If you want to focus on rabbits, great. There are salespeople who make substantial money signing up large volumes of smaller accounts. But I decided early on I wanted to go after fewer clients with larger volumes of business. I wanted to find the rocks with the largest chunks of gold underneath.

The rest of this book will be devoted to giving you the mental and tactical equipment you need to be a successful Sales Hunter. A lot of what I share should feel familiar because most of it's common sense once you become aware of it. The problem is there's been a lot of noise from so-called sales gurus which has obscured this common sense from becoming common practice.

If you learn to hunt and keep your mindset and practices focused on delivering the highest degree of service, you'll grow and excel in your craft. You'll build a business from sales—and you'll be doing it by using your company's overhead instead of having to build it all on your own like an entrepreneur. One day, as you prepare to enter a promising retirement, you might look back and realize sales was the best path to the rich rewards you enjoy.

And guess what? You'll have the satisfaction of knowing you *earned* it.

Having the right tools creates competence. Competence creates confidence. Let's cultivate that competence together now.

CHAPTER 2

TREASURE HUNTING BASICS

One of the keys to deer hunting I learned early on was to look for water, especially streams. All living creatures need a source of water, so naturally, deer can be found near one. And when you're out in the woods for hours on end tracking and on the move, you also might be grateful for the stream if your canteen happens to run dry!

Now imagine the forest stream represents your own wealth and success sitting in front of you. At any moment, you can reach in and the water you pull out is reflective of the wealth flowing into your life.

But let's say you don't have a bowl or cup anywhere in sight, and you'll have to use your hands. You reach into the stream to grab a fistful of water, clinging as tight as you can, afraid to lose even a single drop. Water doesn't respond well to a death grip, though. The tighter you squeeze, the quicker it slips between your fingers.

What if you tried a different approach? What if you adapt, adapt by cupping your hands together as you dip into the stream? You'll find the water is held fast when you draw your hands back out.

Sales can feel this way. Clients will come—and then go just as quickly, along with your commission. Most of the time, it's when you least expect—just when you thought it was your most secure account.

I don't say this to scare you or create paranoia. Instead, it's just a reminder of how the markets we serve are always moving. Ebbing and flowing—like water in a stream.

When it comes to the basics of treasure hunting, we must first understand how *everything* in life ebbs and flows—whether it be yourself, your family, relationships, or professional life. We need to look at sales in the light.

Whether you've been in sales for a few years already or you're just starting your career, it's never too late to return to what you *think* you already know. Examine your knowledge through a fresh lens. You can sit by the stream and complain you don't have a cup. Or you can use what you *do* have—your hands—to take a drink.

But if you can acquire a cup, then by all means, get the cup!

That said, for you to be successful, you need the right tools on hand. Different types of hunting require different tools—and some tools change over time. Our ancestors hunted with bows and arrows. Today, we use rifles. It's the same in sales, so this isn't about discussing every possible scenario you could encounter.

Instead, we're going to chat more about the timeless basics of both your mentality and tactical strategy for Sales Hunting. A lot of the concepts I introduce here are ones we'll return to in more detail later on, but it's important we at least get on the same page with the tried-and-true ways to think about being a Sales Hunter.

TOOL #1: REDEFINE THE COLD CALL.

When I describe what I do, I sometimes get the response, "Mike, that's just cold calling, and everyone knows cold calling is dead. It doesn't work!" First off, a whole other book could be written about whether cold calling is dead, but I think it makes more sense for us to first look at what I mean by "cold call" and redefine it in the context of being a Sales Hunter.

The term "cold calling" has been around longer than most people realize. In fact, the first documented version of a cold call took place in the 1870s by John Patterson, the founder of the National Cash Register Company. He did most of his business face-to-face, but he also created the basic formula many sales professionals still follow for the call scripts we think about when we hear the term "cold calling."[3]

Most people have an idea what cold calling is, and many have even done it even if they don't realize it. To some, the cold call represents the worst aspect of sales: an unsolicited pitch that's a waste of one's time and energy. Plus, for the one doing the cold call, it can be uncomfortable, grueling, and often plagued by rejection. What's there to like about it?

Even just thinking about the term itself might cause you to shudder, and I totally understand why. The answer is in the word: it's *cold*.

I don't like the term personally, which is why this will likely be the only section of the book where you'll see me use it. For me, it conjures up the picture of sitting in a bland cubicle as a computer

---

3   HBS Working Knowledge, "John H. Patterson and the Sales Strategy of the National Cash Register Company, 1884 to 1922," HBS.edu, November 1, 1999, accessed June 8, 2023, https://hbswk.hbs.edu/item/john-h-patterson-and-the-sales-strategy-of-the-national-cash-register-company-1884-to-1922.

randomly dials numbers, hoping someone will pick up and listen to your prewritten script. As I said in the last chapter, it's just "dialing for dollars."

It's a bleak picture. And for me, hunting is the opposite. Hunting means movement. Hunting means intention. Hunting means purpose and drive.

So for our conversation, let's redefine what is meant by the term "cold call." Let's change the narrative. Let's transform it into something warm and worth exploring.

A major reason salespeople are turned off by cold calling is the fear of rejection. But rejection in sales is like the sun coming up every morning. We *know* it's going to happen, whether we like it or not. It may occur less with warm leads, but it still happens—just ask any Sales Farmer if they close 100 percent of the "warm" leads they are fed. I guarantee you they don't.

HUNTING MEANS INTENTION. HUNTING MEANS PURPOSE AND DRIVE.

In other words, rejection is just something you have to get used to. Instead of fearing it, you have to make it part of you, like the clothes you put on every morning.

Instead of looking at cold calling as a rejection machine, what if we looked at it as another building block to create opportunity? Cold calling in the context of a Sales Hunter is all about feeling the room you're in. It's about learning what the client needs, what their problems are. Once you have a clear idea, even if it's a small one, you offer up a solution as an advisor. You find out why the prospect's world is cold—and investigate whether you have a way to warm it up.

In Sales Hunting, cold calling is really about finding an opportunity to expand your business where there was no opportunity before. You can cold call every day without realizing you're even doing it.

Maybe you strike up a conversation with someone waiting in line for coffee, not even trying to sell them anything. By just being human and forming a connection, we can create something from nothing. Even the simple question "So what do you do?" holds immense power to reveal new opportunities.

The stereotypical view of cold calling removes the most important element in sales: being human. If all you've got in your tool belt is a script you recite like a machine, there is no human-to-human connection being made. You're not truly

BY JUST BEING HUMAN AND FORMING A CONNECTION, WE CAN CREATE SOMETHING FROM NOTHING.

listening to what the customer needs or what their problem is. It's a one-sided transaction which leaves people feeling used—and leaves you feeling dejected nine times out of ten.

God gave us two ears and one mouth. It's time to use them proportionately.

By shifting how we view the "cold call" from a disembodied voice on the other end of the phone, to a warm, living human making a connection, it becomes a useful tool. It creates opportunities for growth. It's not something we have to fear or loathe. It just needs to be redefined and seen in its proper context.

TOOL #2: ADAPT OR DIE.

When you're selling a service or product generally regarded as valuable in your market, it's easy to become complacent. This is especially true for Established Hunters. We can become overconfident when we have the brand name on the flag we're carrying. But remember, even the Roman Empire got carved up and disappeared.

You have to remain alert, knowing a change in your industry or product could occur in a split second—and you'll miss it if you're not on the lookout.

Think of it like this: If you were the best blacksmith in town a hundred years ago and made the best horseshoes, you would enjoy some steady success. But then one day, you see the Model T drive by for the first time.

GOD GAVE US TWO EARS AND ONE MOUTH. IT'S TIME TO USE THEM PROPORTIONATELY.

If I had to guess, the Model T was probably met with skepticism and doubt. Maybe some of the other blacksmiths in town say, "It's a fad. It'll never catch on." Or perhaps they become bitter as they watch more Model T's begin to fill the town's roads as their pool of regular customers shrinks.

But you're different. Instead of being bitter or seeing a fad, you see opportunity. Your industry has changed and your customers are flowing in a new direction. You figure, "I learned how to shoe horses. Now I'll learn how to shoe cars." So you go out and acquire some rubber tires.

I learned this lesson firsthand during the bank and housing crisis in 2008. I was working in real estate deals for new construction at the time, and almost overnight, builders were going out of business or pausing work in hopes the crisis would pass fast. If I had only focused on trying to obtain new builder clients, I would've starved or gone out of business myself.

Instead, I asked myself some questions based on my observations. With all the businesses failing in new construction, where was all their "product" going? The empty lots they owned were still there.

The half-built houses weren't vanishing anytime soon. What would happen to these?

Through these questions, I led myself, unknowingly, into a whole new market niche called "receivership." This is where the court takes over the foreclosure process and disposes of the property. I found a way to integrate myself into the process and created opportunities to not just survive the crisis but make more money than I would've made in typical market conditions! Had I sat around moping and groaning like others did, I would've missed out. Good hunters, though, are always observing the conditions around them so they know where to move next.

There are always going to be ups and downs in the market. Like rejection, it's something you just need to accept. Hunters spend less time worrying about what the market is doing and more time figuring out how to be a part of what it's doing. In 2008, I looked for where the business was flowing and found a way to get right in the middle of the stream.

With any crossroad you face, there are two ways you can go. The first way is to figure out where you can fit in the market. Find the new "cultural norm" on the other side of the change by trading in your horseshoes for tires. This requires hard work and diligence to achieve your goals, but it means you stay in business.

The other way is looking for the "easy way" to get the job done. Unfortunately, this is the path which throws ethics out the window. Here, you don't care about what's right or wrong, just getting the money and running. This is where the scam artists land who take advantage of people's problems and are no better than common thieves.

These two paths represent the difference between working hard at a job to buy the car of your dreams—and selling drugs to buy the car of your dreams. The first one comes with the satisfaction of knowing you did it right—you *earned* it. The other carries the risk of ending up in prison and losing everything. I'm stealing this analogy from Tony Robbins, of course, but as he points out, why not use that same level of ambition to do things the right way?

TOOL #3: DON'T GIVE UP.

Remember—it's a treasure hunt. You're standing in a massive field littered with rocks of all different shapes and sizes—and some are hiding gold. You know the gold is there somewhere, but where do you start? How long do you keep looking?

It can feel overwhelming at first, seeing the endless amount of rocks which need to be searched. The first key when overturning some of those rocks, though, is to get in the mindset of *not giving up*. This way, after you turn over three hundred rocks and your hands are dirty

DON'T GIVE UP. DIG IN.

and your back hurts, it doesn't stop you from turning over another three hundred the next day.

Perseverance is a discipline. Don't give up. Dig in. In sales, you can expect to find one golden boulder to live off of for the rest of your life. It's not the lottery—it's a lifestyle. Every rock you turn over, every appointment you go to, what is your goal? Is it to make a sale? Or are you thinking about what you're going to eat afterward?

At every sales appointment, I walk in with the goal of landing a deal. Does it happen every time? Of course not! But when the meeting is over, I immediately analyze what went right and whether I got closer to achieving the deal.

Sometimes you are going to turn over a rock in the field of opportunity and it won't have gold, but it *will* have a clue for where you can find gold. Sometimes you dig and discover another rock blocking your way. It just means you might need to *keep* digging.

Perseverance is about more than "not giving up." It's about having a positive attitude which keeps you moving.

So if I have a meeting and I accomplish *anything* positive, even if it's short of the goal I set, that's what I focus on—the positive. I celebrate the growth. This is what keeps me moving to the next appointment or scheduling the follow-up with the prospect. Think about it: how can you be successful if you only focus on the negatives? Remember the positives and build off of them.

Imagine if you're a professional baseball player and your batting average is .350. With that average, you're one of the best hitters in the entire league. In fact, if you keep this up your entire career, you'd be enshrined in the Hall of Fame next to Ty Cobb.

The same thing applies to sales.

Will you always hit a homerun? No, but you don't need a hit every time you're "at bat" with a prospect. You just need to keep swinging.

If you shift your perspective to one of perseverance, suddenly it's not as discouraging when someone tells you no. It makes rejection more bearable, less overwhelming. We will talk more about the "Power of No" later in the chapter, but for now, just get back into the field of opportunity. Keep picking up those rocks. Keep looking for gold.

To do so, I strongly encourage you to take note of the small victories or positive takeaways so you are better prepared for the next meeting. Take a moment to reflect on what happened in the meeting, what you learned, and actually write it down. Then you can track your progress and improve your "batting average" next time.

I must admit, I haven't always been the best at this in my career. I wish I had been better at taking notes, especially when just starting out with a new prospect. I've mostly relied on my memory and gut instinct during my entire career, but with technology today and CRMs, there are a multitude of resources to make your hunt easier. Have I been successful? Yes. But I probably would've been more successful *faster* had I stopped to take more notes and *not* relied solely on my memory!

TOOL #4: BREAKING THE ICE—FIRST IMPRESSIONS.

So you've found yourself with a new opportunity. Now what?

First things first: you need to break the ice and get to know the client and their business. You don't have to overthink it—simply ask questions.

What is their business? Do they even need your services? Even if they don't, that's not necessarily a loss. Who's to say they won't need it later on? Can they refer you to someone who does? They're going to remember the salesperson who was genuinely interested in them beyond the transaction.

If they are already using a provider for your industry, don't ask, "What does your current provider do?" Instead, ask, "What does your current provider do to make your life great?"

This sounds crazy, I know. You might even be thinking, "Mike, why would I want to get them saying something positive about my competitor?"

But this is a beneficial method for opening the door of opportunity. By asking them what their current provider is already doing well, then it gives you the information for what *you* also need to do well should you earn their business later on. It's also more disarming, takes down the "sales wall," and gets the prospect talking about what makes them excited. All of this is golden information you can convert into a sale.

Before you can do anything else, you have to acknowledge the prospect you are meeting for the first time is judging every aspect of you. As they *should*, since they have no idea who you are. Wouldn't you do the same? As we all know, first impressions can make or break us. Whether it's for a job interview, a first date, or a first sales call, the first time you meet someone leaves a lasting impression.

First impressions *really* matter in sales, but they don't have to be daunting. Think of this stage as establishing your brand. What makes you the best choice? You'll be establishing your reputation and brand throughout the entire process, but these early days are vital because it's the first time they get to see you in person and in action.

Meanwhile, your prospect is *also* on a treasure hunt. They want to find the people and services which make *them* look better. If your brand isn't shiny and rock solid like gold, then they will move on and keep turning over other rocks.

While preparing to write this book, I interviewed multiple business executives, and they all listed the same traits they look for in a sales representative. They want someone who is sincere and confident in their own skin. In other words, when first meeting a potential client, be yourself because when we are ourselves, we have natural confidence. We aren't pretending to be something we aren't. This often speaks louder than words.

A key here: Don't pretend you *aren't* there to get their business. Everyone knows why you're there, but set the expectation you want to get to know them and their business first.

People want to know that if they give you a chance, you are confident and self-motivated enough to make things happen for their business. You're probably not going to know exactly how you'll do this the first time you meet with them, but that's OK.

Sales is an ongoing adventure, so you don't need all the answers right away. What you need is for them to see you will find those answers, no matter what it takes.

The worst move you can make in the sales arena is to predetermine what the client needs from you. Too many salespeople approach prospects with the mindset of, "I'm gonna tell you what we do well, and this is what I'm gonna sell to you." That's like trying to sell tennis shoes to someone looking for snow boots.

Instead, your first action should be to *learn* what your client needs. Engage with them and show a genuine interest. Assuming you know the prospect's needs is a recipe for failure.

When our livelihood is based on commissions, we can easily get caught up in closing a sale and forget to be human. Breaking the ice is about connecting with another person across the table. The focus isn't on what *you* can achieve, but what you can achieve for *them*.

ASSUMING YOU KNOW THE PROSPECT'S NEEDS IS A RECIPE FOR FAILURE.

As important as it is to learn in those early conversations, it doesn't hurt to show you've done your research on their business to learn as much as you can beforehand. When making your introduction either on the phone or in person, you should be communicating the following ideas, even if your exact words are a bit different:

"I'd like to put myself in a position to be one of your providers in the future. I understand you probably already have a provider, so I wouldn't expect you to make any changes unless they do something wrong. But for now, I'd love to start by hearing about your needs so I can share what we can do and can't do. That way, we can be your *alternative* if you ever have a need your provider can't fulfill."

Even if the door is closed, it can still be cracked open for the future because now they know you exist. And if they take you at your word, they might actually give you some business their current provider can't do. Granted, it'll probably be the ugliest, dustiest project they have, but they may offer it up to see if you will rise to the challenge. Sometimes it's their way of saying, "Hey, if you can salvage this, then you have our business."

With sincerity and confidence, executives will see you have their best interests at heart. By being honest and straightforward, people will reward you by keeping in touch, even if the door seems closed at first.

When I'm standing in front of a client for the first time and I tell them what I'm going to do for their business, I say, "You have the benefit of having me as one of *your* employees who, fortunately for you, gets paid by *another* company."

By establishing a solid relationship from the very beginning, your reputation and brand will serve you even after you close the deal—and help you move past any mistakes that may occur. It takes no special talent to cultivate a reputation and brand of sincerity, work ethic, and

IT TAKES NO SPECIAL TALENT TO CULTIVATE A REPUTATION AND BRAND OF SINCERITY, WORK ETHIC, AND DEDICATION.

dedication. Anyone can choose those qualities. Anyone can reap their long-term benefits.

If you position yourself as an advocate for your clients, that's what makes them a fan of yours. They'll stick with you through thick and thin. In fact, there was a client I worked with once who had a financial dispute with our company, and they were prepared to take it to court. Because I had invested early on in the relationship to play the middleman representing everybody at the table, we were able to resolve the issue peaceably. More details on this later when we discuss nurturing relationships!

The point is this: Even after the dispute, I never once lost a deal with them. They were correct, there was an error, and we found a resolution. So once the dust settled, we were then able to show how much we valued their business, and they allowed us to move forward in our business relationship. None of this would've been possible if I hadn't invested early on in breaking the ice with a strong first impression.

TOOL #5: TWO-WAY FLOW.

The entire sales process is a two-way street, or what I like to call a "two-way flow," especially in the early days of getting to know a client. Not only are they deciding if you are the right fit for them, but you should ask yourself the same question! Are they the right client for *you*?

To discover whether a prospect is worth your time, there are a couple of key questions you should keep track of in your notes:

Are they being sincere and honest with the information they tell you?

Can you realistically work with them—or are they demanding too much?

There are more questions, of course, which I will address later on, but by actively listening and engaging with the client, you'll have a good idea of whether the lead is truly warm or if you're wasting your time.

So what are some signs you should know to both protect yourself and learn if the lead is worth pursuing?

The first is a double-edged sword and easily overlooked: If you're able to talk a prospect out of an existing provider with one call or meeting, how easy will it be for your competition to come in and do the same? If a client makes big lofty decisions with little to no evidence they need to make a change, then you can assume they will do the same to you as well.

So sure, you'll get their business for a few months. It's a short-term win, but are they someone you want to be partnered with long term?

Probably not.

After talking with the client for a bit, try to learn the following:

First, are they doing business with your competition?

Second, have they contacted your company before and started a relationship with any of your peers?

Both of these are important questions you need answered before you can even begin to think about a follow-up meeting or next steps. Why?

If they are in business with your competition and *not* being entertained by someone else within your company, then it's safe to continue moving forward with your discussions. If they have already begun discussions with a peer from your company, I would recommend allowing your peer the opportunity to close the deal they already started. If you gain a reputation in your company for poaching prospects from your fellow salespeople, it will catch up to you. No one will want to work with you on the really big accounts where more than one rep is required. Or when you want to take a once-in-a-lifetime trip where you'll be out of pocket—who's going to want to sub in for you for the customer service calls?

To put it simply, a balance has to be struck during this process. The client has every right to judge you, but you need to be judging them at the same time. If a meeting turns sour, at least from what you are learning about them, then guess what? That's also a positive! You probably saved yourself a future headache and unneeded stress from a bad client.

TOOL #6: FOLLOW UP OR LOSE OUT.

I always tell my clients, "If you ever call or text me and I don't respond fairly soon, I either overlooked it, or I am dead—and the second is more likely because I take your needs that seriously."

Availability is an underrated value in sales. Keep in mind, this depends on where you are at in the sales process. Are you still in the early days, or have you established a relationship? For our purposes here, let's just assume we are still in the early days—they are considering your offer but have not decided to give you the deal yet. In this case, then your follow-up process should start *before* you leave the first meeting.

What do I mean?

Follow their lead by asking what follow-up works best for them: "Do you prefer email, phone call, or another in-person meeting?" Remember, be sincere and authentic all the way through. Asking for their follow-up preference scores you points for putting their interests first.

You don't want to be the one who checks in once every day and is extra pushy. No one is ever going to do business with that person.

But you also don't want to be the one who *never* goes back and never gets the business because you never asked for it! They'll assume you forgot about them and moved on to "better" prospects. Silence is communication too!

It's a very fine line between these two, which you have to judge case by case. There's no preset formula to follow. You have to be aware of your audience and read the room to determine when you're spending either too much or too little time.

In conversations with many of my clients, one of the first things they'll usually scoff at is how salespeople make themselves too much of an annoyance. Remember: We need to be there to make their day *better*, not *longer*.

A rule I like to follow is devoting my Fridays to one of two activities: admin or fun. Unless I'm *specifically* asked to do something or a problem arises on a Friday, I don't do it. Instead, I either catch up on administrative tasks or I take people to lunch, play golf, and have fun with clients. I do both if possible. But Friday afternoon at three o'clock is *not* the time to show up at a client's office to talk to them about giving you business.

Their purpose for working all week isn't *you*. They want to get out of the office and go see their family. If you burst onto the scene on Friday afternoon, you are now a distraction. Not a helpful hand.

TOOL #7: SOLVE PROBLEMS.

You're going to make mistakes, and problems are going to happen. It's not a matter of *if*, but *when*. Unfortunately, a bad habit I've seen among many salespeople is they like to ignore the problems and do the fun stuff first. If you wake up and see two messages, one from a customer who wants to go golfing and the other from a client who is upset with a pricing error, which one should you respond to first?

It's common sense, but humans routinely ignore common sense, don't we?

More often than not, people will take the free golf day and leave the problem for later. Like I said in the previous section, there is time for fun, but when a problem is knocking at your door, you have to answer it first. Remember—sales is about solving problems. If you're not solving a problem for them, then why should they keep you around?

I've learned that if I don't deal with a problem right away, it easily builds negative momentum. Like a snowball rolling down a mountain, it gets bigger and bigger, faster and faster. Pretty soon, the little snowball becomes an avalanche with the velocity to destroy anything in its path—including your relationship with your best client.

Instead, stop the momentum before it even begins. Turn the problem into another opportunity. What most in sales don't realize is how you are earning a future deal when there is a problem. Sure, it might feel like hell at the moment, but if you can show you care about their problem, then you build trust—and you build your brand. When you solve problems for your clients, even if they don't like the proposed solution right away, it is a great catalyst for establishing a strong relationship and respect for the future.

Practically speaking, never commit to any sort of plan in front of the customer. As salespeople, we know how to talk, and sometimes we can talk too much. Or is it just me?

This can be a fatal mistake if an issue arises. If we over-talk or overpromise before we have any real idea of what to do, we set ourselves up for failure. To put it simply, less is more. Take the issue back to your employer first, then lay out a solid blueprint to find a solution that works for everyone involved. Along the way, make sure to update the client on the steps you're taking, even if you're waiting for an answer from somebody. These are all small actions you can take to build more trust.

A peer shared with me the following story, which expresses "the less is more" way of thinking perfectly. A few years back, he and his sales partner were out proposing a deal to a large oil and gas company, who, at the time, had a giant chunk of land they were getting ready to sell to builders. My peer's partner struck up a casual conversation about how much he loved driving his electric car and how much money he was saving by not buying gas. Not the best time to do this, right?

My peer was obviously furious with his partner's lack of awareness. No one working at the oil and gas company wanted to hear about his EV. At best, they probably thought my peer and his partner were idiots, and at worst, they asked themselves, "Why in the world would we give them our business?" As I said, sometimes, we can talk *too* much in sales, and we need to learn to listen more.

A solution to what our client needs could be sitting right in front of us, just like the stream representing your wealth and success from the opening of this chapter. If we aren't cautious, we can let any opportunity slip through our fingers.

A good hunter doesn't wander around aimlessly but already has an idea of where to go. When I go hunting, we scout out specific areas where the animals we're looking for can normally be found. Do we always find them right away? No. You have to stay light on your feet, always prepared to change on the fly.

I first read *The Art of War* by Sun Tzu fifteen years ago and read it cover to cover. I believe it's the first truly great management book since so many of its lessons can be transferred to everyday life. For example, it teaches how the actual engagement into conflict happens when the plan falls apart. When you go to war, you have the best plans and contingencies, but it can all change instantly. It's when the plan goes awry that you can really shine.

Former Navy SEALs have written about how in the heat of battle, when the bullets start flying, the plan goes out the window. It becomes time to react and adapt, no matter how thorough the plan was. This doesn't mean you don't have a plan at all—it just means you have to stay nimble. The same goes with solving problems. As new ones develop, be ready to react.

TOOL #8: THE POWER OF NO.

Let's end these basics with a real-life example that combines most of the basic treasure hunting methods here. What's ironic is how this all started with getting a "No" from a prospect.

A few years ago, I had a client who kept telling me they were not interested in my offering. But I didn't give up, because I knew what I could offer in service and delivery would give them a much better experience. I did my research and knew the competition, their product offerings, and their salespeople. I knew who was supplying them with their overall experience. I knew what they needed, and I was determined for them to know, too.

I can distinctly recall the quandary as I considered my approach. I couldn't challenge their belief they were already receiving the best possible service. To do so would've looked petty at best. At worst, it would've been equivalent to telling them, "Hey, you made a bad business decision." No one wants to hear that even if they know it's true. I had to come up with a better, more careful way.

So I waited for my opportunity.

You see, there's always going to be an opportunity somewhere down the line. People leave jobs, retire from jobs—or your competitor starts doing a bad job because they get complacent. There are a lot of different circumstances that can create opportunities for someone new to step in. If you pay attention to what's going on, you can step in and earn their business.

For three years, I met with the client on a quarterly basis to review how things were going for them. I continued to verbally support their decision to remain with their service provider, only suggesting I could be their "backup" option. I listened to their concerns and took time to show them I was simply on their team.

Finally, the opportunity I was waiting for came. A key individual at my competition was retiring—the escrow officer who oversaw all of the operational aspects of the transactions. For my prospect, this was going to have a detrimental impact on the services they were receiving.

It was time to go hunting.

They had been forthright and forthcoming in telling me exactly how they want to be treated as a client, so when the time came, I was prepared. In those three years of waiting, I listened intently and gained trust over time. When I struck, I called them up and said, "Hey, I have a solution for you!"

In the face of this brand-new operational problem, I presented them with a solution that resolved all their stress *before* any crisis arose. I committed to a smooth transition, using all the information I had gathered over the years, showing I could provide the level of service they expected without missing a beat.

The best part about this story is that the client is still as loyal to me ten years later as they were at the start. They are one of my most loyal clients and give me everything they can despite some minor glitches along the way. There will always be some minor glitches, but we've worked through every one of them without ever experiencing a hiccup in our relationship.

There is power in getting a "no."

There is also power when you miss the "perfect shot" when hunting.

Something shifts inside and urges you to try again, to keep searching for the next big find, the next shot you can take. You can use a "no" or a missed shot to empower yourself and get better at what you do.

Or as I did with this particular "no," you can leverage it to gain the information you need. This way, when opportunities present themselves down the road, you are armed with the knowledge about what they need for their business to succeed. By the time the need arises, you have prepared yourself to help them achieve their goals in a format they have already spelled out for you. It removes the guesswork.

If you learn one thing from this book, commit this to memory: "No" is not indifference. In fact, "No" should always be treated as a call for more information. They're telling you they want to know "the why," so help them understand why you are the right salesperson for them, why your company, and why they can only get this level of commitment from someone like you who is invested in *their* future.

HOW YOU THINK IS HOW YOU ACT

We'll return to all of these concepts throughout the rest of the book, but if you can begin practicing these basics of treasure hunting, you'll begin to see some immediate results. Remember, your mental strategy influences your tactical strategy and vice versa. The way you think is the way you act. Think selfishly about your own goals, and your prospects will see it in how you act. Think about what they need out of the relationship, and it will show.

Once you establish this kind of thought process, when you can approach clients sincerely and confidently, you can become an unstoppable force focused on achieving *their* stated business goals. When their need is your primary focus, you will be the person who is always out there bringing in the new business.

You might be thinking, "That's great, Mike. But how do I even get the first call? How do I start breaking the ice with the decision-maker if there's someone else in my way?" To that, I'd say, "You're right. Sales is rarely just a conversation between two people." Who else is involved in the process? Who are the gatekeepers you need to open the gate of opportunity?

CHAPTER 3

THE GATEKEEPERS

When you think of gatekeepers, what comes to mind? Maybe you picture a giant medieval fortress with guards patrolling the battlements, on the lookout for enemies. Throughout history, gatekeepers have played an essential role in society, entrusted to keep communities safe and secure. In many ways, this is still true.

Granted, today's gatekeepers may not have a sword or spear in hand. Instead, they might be sitting at a desk, armed with a laptop and phone. Whether it's the lobby receptionist or the executive assistant, these company gatekeepers don't dictate your life or death, but it might feel like it at times. How you treat and interact with gatekeepers will help determine—and even direct—your success in sales.

At first glance, you might not think the gatekeeper is important. After all, you aren't there to see them—you're there to talk to the decision-maker (DM), whether it's the COO, the vice president, or whatever "big" title they have. It's easy to be so focused on how you're going to engage with the DM, you neglect to consider your interaction with the gatekeeper.

But guess what?

Your meeting with the DM begins as soon as you approach the front desk. Without the gatekeeper, it is nearly impossible to do your job. Remember, first impressions matter, and in many cases, the gatekeepers you encounter will dictate those first impressions.

The gatekeeper is often the first person who will judge if you are a person worthy of their boss's attention—or if you will waste their time. Their job is to protect the DM's time, and most of them take this job seriously—as they should since it's their job. How they perceive you isn't everything, but why not leverage their influence to your advantage?

THE POWER OF PERCEPTION

Have you ever thought about how your perceptions shape your decisions in day-to-day life? We all perceive the world based on the clues available to us. For example, let's say you're walking down the street and see a disheveled gentleman headed toward you who looks a bit frayed and tattered.

What would be the first three things to pop into your mind?

Maybe his appearance strikes you as looking dangerous. You might consider whether he has a substance abuse problem. Maybe or maybe not. You don't know until you get to know him. But in just a few brief moments, a perception of the individual could lead you to reach a false conclusion.

What if I told you he was the most successful gentleman in town? That he owns most of the real estate in town but was volunteering at the local veteran's hospital, helping pull weeds in the garden and that's why he looks so disheveled? This changes your perception, doesn't it?

We all make presumptions like this. Your prospects will make presumptions about you when you walk into their office for the first time. While making assumptions isn't fair, it's a part of how we all make choices. As the frontline of the business, this should give us more insight into the gatekeeper's job and the power of how they perceive us.

When you walk into a prospective client's office for the first time, you have to think about what your appearance and demeanor communicates. Does it communicate you're trustworthy? Arrogant? Confident? To some degree, you *can* influence their perception of you and gain credibility, moving you closer to the deal you're hunting for.

One of your goals is to make clients and prospects feel at ease around you. But it's also important to shape a perception you are capable, armed with the skills they need to be successful in their business. More than the product or service your company sells, you sell *yourself*—that is, whether you have the skills, capacity, and expertise to get their problems solved to make their lives easier to manage. If you succeed, you won't have to keep rebuilding your business on a day-to-day basis.

For example, I have a friend in real estate who deals a lot with rental homes. After meeting with a potential renter, he always finds a way to walk them back to their car. He doesn't care what kind of car they drive, but he *is* interested in how the inside of their car looks.

Does it look like a mobile garbage dump? Or is it clean and cared for?

He gains more insight into how the prospective renter will treat his property by observing their car compared to the hour-long conversation they just had.

Think of your interactions with gatekeepers the same way. How you present yourself and how you treat others matters. If you treat the receptionist the same way you treat the DM, this goodwill goes a long way. A good manager will seek their assistant's input even after meeting with you. So if you were a little rude or short with the gatekeeper as you walked in, you can bet the gatekeeper will volunteer the information to the manager when asked, which might sway them to take their business elsewhere.

Gatekeepers can have incredible influence not only in the process of breaking the ice, but over the long term of your business with the client. Case in point, my wife started her career as a gatekeeper and worked her way up to be a top executive. Imagine if I had walked into her office when she was a receptionist and ignored her or was short with her. She would *not* have forgotten it, and if I tried to get her business years later when she was an executive, she would remember me as "that rude guy."

Who we are doesn't change. We can act and pretend to be someone we are not, but at the end of the day, we are still the same person *inside*. When you interact with anyone in a company, their business is always on the line. With each interaction, you have an opportunity to show them how seriously you will take their business—especially with the gatekeeper.

WHEN YOU INTERACT WITH ANYONE IN A COMPANY, THEIR BUSINESS IS ALWAYS ON THE LINE.

As I mentioned earlier, most DMs are looking for sincerity and confidence that you are the person who can solve their problems, not bring more problems to their doorstep.

Knowing this, why would they want to sign a deal with someone who is rude to one of their valued team members? What's your message going to be? That you don't care about them and their company? Or that you'll go the extra mile for them when they need it? You gain nothing by being dismissive of the gatekeeper's influence. You have everything to gain by showing them how valuable they are to the company—and to you.

NAVIGATING THROUGH GATEKEEPERS

Earlier in my career, I dealt with a hostile gatekeeper. His last name was the same as the owner of the business—probably not a coincidence. This told me that gaining access to the DM would be more challenging than usual. Still, I knew their business needs, and I believed our product would benefit them greatly even though they were already using a different provider.

The first couple of times I went to their office, this gatekeeper gave me the workaround. He'd shut me down right at the door and tell me my contact was busy on the phone and couldn't meet with me. One day, I gently pushed back and said, "OK, that's fine. Do you know how long he will be on the phone?" The gatekeeper just said, "It'll be a while."

Lucky for me, I had exactly "a while" of time on my hands that day, and I was determined to at least get an initial conversation with my contact. I knew there was a courtyard outside, so I took a seat there to wait before trying again. The courtyard worked to my advantage because it just happened to overlook my contact's office, where I could actually see him on the phone inside. I knew better than to just sit and stare like a creep, so I took out my phone to answer emails, occasionally glancing over to see if he was still busy.

After a few more minutes, I glanced over again—and saw my contact standing at the window looking at me. I waved—and he waved back! The door of opportunity which was locked a few minutes before was now cracked open. I went back to the front entrance and asked the gatekeeper if my contact was available now. As a credit to him, he went back and checked, then came back with the answer I wanted to hear: "Yes, he will see you."

Did I get the sale that day? No. But I got to have a real conversation and establish a relationship where I was welcome to stop by every so often. Eventually, there were some changes, their circumstances changed, and I was able to present my solution. In the end, they became a big client of mine.

And as for the gatekeeper? He's become an ardent supporter.

Now, I know this example may seem extreme to some. Not everyone's comfortable with loitering in another company's courtyard. But it was open to the public, so I wasn't trespassing, and the DM chose to wave me in. So how much is *too* much when it comes to creating an opportunity for yourself? Often, you have to determine this *for yourself* on a case-by-case basis.

In this instance, I felt what I did was still respectful, and I didn't force anyone to do anything. I just made sure I was in the right place at the right time since previous attempts hadn't worked. Sometimes you have to figure out where "the line" is with each prospect because it's not going to be the same for everyone. Obviously, me waving from the courtyard was fair game for this DM.

One day, you may find yourself in a similar situation and you'll have to feel out where the line is. Many times, it can feel like the gatekeeper is deciding where "the line" is, which is where it can become frustrating. So the question to answer is how do you get *around* a gatekeeper if they are locking you out?

Most of the time, you won't have to if you're being respectful, nice, and courteous. They're good people who are just doing their job. Continuing to do *my* job means I keep showing up, not getting upset, and not showing any kind of indignation when they tell me I can't see the DM. Eventually, their barriers and hesitations will start to break down when I can show myself as an ally.

For starters, don't be afraid to *ask* the gatekeeper for help. If it feels like you've hit a dead-end, like in my story above, then simply ask for help or more clarity:

> "I wanted to see if you could help me. I know the DM is busy and you know *far* better than I do what's best for them, so how do they prefer to set up appointments? Do you handle it? Do they prefer email? A lunch invitation? What do you think?"

Again, never be rude or offensive—even if you already set an appointment that has conveniently disappeared from the schedule. In fact, if that happens, even better, because you can showcase your flexibility and willingness to work with them:

> "Oh, they need to reschedule? I understand—they have a big job. Can you help me out with rescheduling or is it best for me to reach back out to them directly?"

Asking for a gatekeeper's help and expertise is generally a great way to disarm any hostility they might harbor due to past interactions with pushy salespeople. Since their job is to help others, you're actually asking them to do something that triggers a *positive* response for them.

Still, if you feel like no progress is being made and you're starting to waste your time and resources, here are some questions to help you keep moving forward after being blocked for the thousandth time:

"Is there a better time of day for me to stop by? Can I set up a time in advance with you now? Is there an email address I should use instead?"

These are great follow-up questions to attain more clarity, and invites the gatekeeper to help solve the situation alongside you. It puts you both on the same team as you try to set a time that works for everyone. The gatekeeper will appreciate this since it gives them a sense of control about when you'll pop in next, rather than surprise them on an inconvenient day.

DON'T BE AFRAID TO ASK THE GATEKEEPER FOR HELP.

By starting an honest dialogue, asking polite follow-up questions, and remaining respectful, they'll also help clue you in about how the DM likes to do business. Repeated denials for access can be frustrating, but always remember, they are *just doing their job*, too! Good gatekeepers also recognize part of the DM's day is to talk to new service providers because they never know when they might need a change or find a better deal.

But let's say you encounter the rare gatekeeper who is simply unmovable and unrelenting despite all your best efforts. FAIR WARNING: This one is much riskier because it's a last-ditch effort. But one strategy is to literally move around the gatekeeper's day. If you notice they take their lunch around noon, then guess what time you should show up? That's right, noon. If you discover they don't work on Mondays, then you show up on Monday.

Again, this is risky because you could possibly fracture the relationship with the company right at the start, especially if the gatekeeper finds out you've sidestepped them for access to their boss. This can make *them* look bad, frustrate their boss, and now you've created a deeper obstacle when trying to manage the relationship, even if they give you their business. They might never let go of the grudge, so I would say to use this strategy *sparingly*.

I've used this strategy before myself, which is why I am offering it up. Just know it *can* easily backfire on you. In fact, it's backfired on me before! Leaving a damaged or hurt individual behind will often come back to haunt you. If you make enemies within an organization, you can count on them working to get rid of you the first chance they get. Even if the hostile gatekeeper is far removed from the DM, if they don't like you as a person and don't respect your way of doing business, they will gladly magnify any problems that arise.

In other words, this is a "Hail Mary" pass. Use it only as a last resort when you know you're on your final attempt. At a certain point, you have to ask yourself, "Is it worth my time and energy to continue trying to see this prospect? Or would my time and energy be spent on someone else?"

If it works out for you, then great. If it doesn't, then just move on to the next rock you need to search under.

A good best practice: If you want to do business with XYZ Company, then consider *everybody* who works for XYZ Company as a decision-maker, whether or not you continue to do business with them. Treat everyone with the same respect and things will go far smoother.

A WELL OF INFORMATION

As obvious as this sounds, it needs to be said: the best way to set yourself up for success is to establish great rapport with the gatekeeper.

This doesn't happen overnight, but once you are in a good place, the gatekeeper can become a well of information for you. For instance, let's say you've been managing an account for a year and it's been going great. Then one day, you pick up on some slight hesitation from the DM. If you have established a healthy, positive relationship with the gatekeeper, you might ask them, "Hey, has anyone else been coming in lately?"

Nine times out of ten, they will give you the scoop. Sometimes without you even asking, they will give you a heads-up because if they like you, they'd rather keep seeing *you* than start over with another company's rep. The cold hard truth in sales is, once you think you are comfortable with an account, you're most likely on the way out. That's why building relationships matter, as we'll discuss more soon.

Gatekeepers can be great allies when you need them, and there have been many cases where they told me they denied a rival company or they listened to an hour-long presentation from my competition and told them "no." That information is as good as gold because it's a warning others are trying to steal away your hard-earned treasure. Now, if you don't have a good relationship with the gatekeeper, do you think they'll tell you *anything*?

Not at all.

When they're on your side, gatekeepers can become part of your own defense. If they like you, they can (and will) provide you with critical information about your competitor. If they don't like you, they will gladly feed information to your competition. They'll be the last person to shoot a fiery arrow into your heart when they cancel your contract.

THE EXECUTIVE ASSISTANT

When it comes to the types of gatekeepers you interact with, executive assistants hold a little more weight than most. The biggest difference between a typical gatekeeper—like a receptionist—and an executive assistant is their power to help with setting the DM's schedule. Where the receptionist likely has no access to the DM's calendar, the executive assistant may know the DM's schedule better than the DM.

First and foremost, always speak to the executive assistant with the same sincerity and respect you would show the executive. Also, make it a point to tell them the "why" behind the meeting so they can schedule out the correct time needed. Failing to pay attention to this detail means you could end up with a fifteen-minute block for a conversation that really requires an hour. That's not their fault, it's yours! You can't expect them to read your mind, and you can't expect the executive to clear their schedule for you at a moment's notice.

Also, by setting clear expectations, you might discover there needs to be more than one DM present. The executive assistant might say, "Oh, in that case, you should meet on Thursday, because that's when they have their weekly update with Operations who would need to weigh in on this too." This can greatly shorten the time it takes to close the deal by getting the right people into the right room at the right time.

You have to remember the DM has a high level of trust with their executive assistant, which is why they were selected for the job. They see the ins and outs of the executive's schedule and life, which extends their authority in many ways. If they don't trust you, then the boss won't trust you either.

There's a simple reason the DM has an assistant handling their personal affairs and schedule. It's because they don't have enough time to do it themselves. You should assume they have been working together for a *long* time. Even if it's not true, this assumption works to your benefit as you talk to the executive assistant as someone who has knowledge of the business itself. Knowing this, I would caution *never* sidestepping the executive assistant—not if you actually want to do business with the company.

THE GOLDEN RULE

I know I'm sounding like a broken record here, but if there is one thing to remember from this chapter, it's that no business happens without establishing a relationship first. We will talk much more about the importance of relationships in the following chapter, but the relevance here with gatekeepers is key to your success as a Sales Hunter. Treating others how you would like to be treated is the first step in getting your foot in the door. It's the Golden Rule not just in life, but in sales, too. Believe me, I understand it can be difficult, especially with gatekeepers who like to hide the key or throw it away altogether.

You'll quickly discover such people are outliers, not the constants. They either don't last because they're hostile to everyone or they may even indicate the company culture itself is hostile and not worth your effort. But for the most part, the gatekeepers on the frontline should be your best friends! You want them to know you as respectful and genuine. Also, it never hurts to learn their favorite coffee order and bring it in on your next visit!

Treat gatekeepers like the diamonds they are and they will return your investment by becoming the segue into financial security for yourself and your family. Bring them along on your journey to your goals. Depending on *how* you treat them, gatekeepers can be either building blocks or roadblocks.

CHAPTER 4

NURTURING RELATIONSHIPS

You might be sick and tired of hearing me mention how important relationships are in sales, but I will not apologize, because without establishing relationships, sales is like hunting without ammunition.

Can you imagine?

You get up at three in the morning to grab your gear bag and head out the door. Maybe you drive an hour away to a secluded site, hike miles to a spot you've scouted before, track for hours—until finally a buck peers its head out from the brush and cautiously makes its way across the clearing in front of you.

You've never seen a buck like this before. It's massive and beautiful. So you steady your excited breath, aim your weapon, line up your shot and—*Click*.

Nothing happens.

The buck's ears perk up as it realizes where you are. Before you can even blink, it's long gone, vanishing in the thick trees.

How frustrating would that be?

Making sure you have everything you need before going hunting is a basic principle—just common sense, right? But this one time, you forgot to double-check your ammunition, and now the perfect buck is gone.

The industry and product knowledge you have is like your hunting weapon of choice—rifle, crossbow—whatever. It's what arms you to go out and actually close the deal. But a weapon is worth nothing if it doesn't have ammo.

Establishing a relationship and connection in sales is a process—each interaction is like stocking up on your ammunition. If you don't take the time to "stock up" before pulling the trigger on a deal, nothing will happen—except startling your prospect so they run off into the woods, never to be seen again.

Here's the thing—no one cares how much you know until they know how much you care.

Nobody wants to do business with someone who is just after their money. People can smell the reek of "commission breath" from a mile away, like a skunk driving away a predator on its tail. Don't be like a skunk. You want to draw the customer *in*. You want to entice them with a fresh opportunity to do business with someone who is genuinely looking out for *their* best interests. That's what relationships are—looking out for the interests of someone besides yourself.

NO ONE CARES HOW MUCH YOU KNOW UNTIL THEY KNOW HOW MUCH YOU CARE.

This is not an original thought, but it's a great one to remember: it's OK to remind an established client or prospect, "I'm on your team, but fortunately for you, I'm being paid by my company." You have to start thinking of yourself as a zero-cost employee for them, ready to handle their interests. That's how I approach all my clients.

Like everything else in sales, there are steps and techniques to establish a solid relationship with your clients and prospects. I shared a few of the basics in the previous chapters, but let's get more specific and focus on how you can "pull the trigger" to land life-changing opportunities by building relationships.

AVAILABILITY IS THE BEST ABILITY

One Friday afternoon, I was walking my dog, looking forward to the weekend. I suddenly received a phone call from a newer client—overall, a pretty small account. For the next hour, I sat on the curb and talked with him about a problem that had cropped up.

Before the conversation ended, I made it a point to ask: "How many other title reps take your call at four o'clock in the afternoon on a Friday?"

They chuckled and responded, "None."

Seeing my opportunity, I asked, "Then how come I don't have all of your business?"

They replied, "That's a great question, Mike."

By simply being the only one willing to take the call on a Friday afternoon, I created a major opportunity to double my business with a new client. Shortly after this exchange, I became his only provider—and my competition was "fired." Availability is the best ability in sales.

AVAILABILITY IS THE BEST ABILITY IN SALES.

Listen, I know it can be tough to respond to phone calls when we get busy. Sales can be overwhelming with a lot of moving pieces, and with the pace of life moving a thousand miles an hour, the phone ringing can feel like just another noise atop a mountain of noise ringing in your ears.

What can you do?

First, understand when a client reaches out to you, they are making a statement to both you and themselves that they see you as a critical part of their team. They are seeking your input. They need your advice. By taking the call, even when it seems like there is nothing you can offer, you are letting them know you *are* a critical part of their journey to success.

So—to put it simply—*take the call.*

Take the call even when you don't feel like it because you never know what opportunity will arise by being available. If you're working when it seems no one else is, you gain positive momentum with your client. You build your brand, establish a reputation, and stand out.

Consider the opposite: What happens if you *don't* take the call? The client doesn't know when you are busy, or tired, or whatever else might be happening in your life. All they care about when they pick up the phone to call you is solving their problem.

I know it doesn't seem like a fair trade, but your problem can never be the client's problem. And their problem always needs to become your problem. That's the challenge in it, and it's a big reason not every salesperson finds success. But each time you answer the call, you add to your ammunition.

> **YOUR PROBLEM CAN NEVER BE THE CLIENT'S PROBLEM. AND THEIR PROBLEM ALWAYS NEEDS TO BECOME YOUR PROBLEM.**

If you decide to ignore the call and wait a day—or more—to follow up, then you leave the door wide open for your competition to step through. It's not rocket science.

I understand that, as humans, we can't be on call 24/7. I'm also not saying every time your phone rings, drop whatever you're doing and serve your client's needs over your family's needs. But I would recommend, if you can't take the call immediately, then follow up in the next possible moment.

This even applies to emails. Cards on the table: sometimes I fail to follow my own advice. I had a client once send me an email, and I didn't take immediate action, so guess what happened? It fell off my list. A day or so went by, and the client called me to ask, "Hey, what's going on with the issue I emailed you about?"

I quickly realized what had happened. Instead of mentioning the thousand other things happening in my week, I simply took full responsibility for the oversight, apologized, and said, "I'll get it done right now."

My personal reputation and brand allowed me some wiggle room with the client, who was more than understanding with me. No one is perfect. In fact, the last time I thought I was perfect, I tried walking across the pool, and I got awfully wet.

Your clients won't expect perfection. By simply being transparent with them, the relationship can actually grow stronger—even through mishaps. This client knew ignoring an email wasn't my regular MO because I'd built up lots of ammunition in the past through quick responses. Still, the sooner you get back to solving *their* needs, the more solidified your position will be moving forward.

The reason I believe in this one principle so much is because my future was changed by simply taking a call on a Thursday evening. A client reached out with a brief window to solve a particular problem. Once I had all the information, I jumped on the phone with my peers to find a solution. Even though it was long after closing hours, the team came together, and a couple of hours later, we had the solution for them. On the same night I was given the problem, I could provide positive news to the client, who was beyond thrilled.

The next morning, we closed a thirteen-million-dollar deal with them.

The best part comes from what I learned *after* we closed the deal. The client told me that several months earlier, they had purposefully *stopped* using my company's services and used a competitor. Before reaching out to me, our competitor failed to answer the call. So my efforts on *their* behalf demonstrated they had my full attention, and whatever they needed, whenever they needed it, I was on their team to make things happen.

Thirteen-million-dollar kinds of things.

PROVIDING VALUE BEFORE A DEAL

Before any relationship begins, whether it's professional or personal, what do we usually look for in the other person?

We look for value.

Not necessarily materialistic value, but we ask ourselves a series of judgment questions. Such as, "What makes this person so special? Are they kind, smart, funny, generous?" The list can include whatever it is we want in a friend, spouse, business partner, or client. But the one common denominator is that we are searching for some kind of value. That's OK, because the person on the other end of the conversation is doing the same, asking what makes *you* so special!

In sales, we can prove our worth *before* we strike any deal. But a common question haunting many salespeople is, "How can we provide value before we are even servicing the customer?" It's a good question and one we must ask ourselves before going into a first meeting with a potential client.

One time, I was standing in a store, minding my own business, when a stranger came up and asked me about a product on sale as if I were in charge.

Have you experienced anything similar?

I have had total strangers assume I was a doctor, a police officer, a store manager, and a long list of other titles. For a long time, I was curious *why* this kept happening to me. Then one day, I figured it out.

I always stand tall, head up, confident in who I am. People are naturally drawn to individuals who are comfortable in their environment and confident in their own skin.

You see, you can provide value just by being comfortable with what you do and how you get your job done. My outward demeanor is one that communicates, "I solve problems. Just let me know what you need." Once I realized this is one of my natural assets, I put it to work in my life every day. If I can establish the perception I am an expert in my field, then why would prospects choose to use my competition?

"THEIR PERCEPTION HAS TO BECOME MY REALITY."

It all goes back to the power of perception. This simple phrase needs to be the mindset of every successful sales professional: "Their perception has to become my reality."

Believe in yourself as an expert and people will naturally see you in the same light.

If you carry yourself like an expert, it doesn't mean you *have* to know everything. In fact, you shouldn't. When you're looking to provide value before a deal is even done, you have to do your research. Try to discover what their business is all about so you have a foundation to build on.

The real learning begins when you have an actual conversation. My approach through this process is to figure out what keeps someone up at night. What are the pesky little problems gnawing at their mind early in the morning? What results will make them look good to their boss? If you can discover those issues and provide a realistic solution for them, you have already provided more value than you can imagine.

Through conversation, learn how—or even *if*—your service/product can benefit and integrate into their company's plethora of needs. The key in all of this is to actually *listen* to them. Listen to learn. Let them tell you their view because your opinion isn't important until they ask for it. Until then, the only opinions that matter about their business are their own. Only after you listen can you earn the privilege to discuss any areas of their business that can benefit from your product or service.

This shouldn't have to be said, but *don't lie about it either!*

Be brutally honest if the service you provide might not be better than the one they are already using. Tell them!

Why?

Because it's an opportunity to provide value to them—even if it means telling them they're already getting the best deal available. It allows you to position yourself as an ally since there is no immediate benefit to you. Who do you think they are going to turn to when their current provider fails to answer the call or makes a big mistake?

YOUR OPINION ISN'T IMPORTANT UNTIL THEY ASK FOR IT.

They will appreciate the honesty and see you're not leading them down a path to nowhere. Because if you know something problematic about the integration of their business with yours, but choose to sweep it under the rug or ignore it, then you're setting yourself up for heartbreak and a lot of stress.

It's like knowing you're going to get a flat tire if you keep driving down a road littered with nails and debris instead of turning around to find a clearer path.

Honesty alone provides value because you're not wasting anyone's time. In fact, this may open their ears up more to hear what *else* you can provide. Start by acknowledging any weak points, then call out the areas of strength. Allow *them* to dictate and define the value you just put on the table for them to see.

It might sound something like this: "Here's an area where this can get tricky, but here are some solutions and contingencies we have in the event of any problems."

In other words, we aren't there to show them how to be better at their business. If a chef showed up at a sales meeting and told you how to do your job better, how would you feel?

The same thing applies to us.

Even if you feel like you fully understand the client's industry, use your ears to listen before using your mouth to speak. Otherwise, you might end up talking yourself into unnecessary problems. It's not about what you want—it's about what *they* need. This might be difficult for some to manage, but again, it's like every other relationship. If you put the needs of your client above your own, they will value the effort and reciprocate in the form of a healthy and stable professional relationship.

Our goal is to form genuine connections and make a living while doing it.

SUIT UP AND SHOW UP

Now, the question we all want to master is, "How do you keep those connections healthy?" After all, business is business, and the sales industry is as cutthroat as they come.

After you close a deal, it doesn't mean you can put up your feet and open a cold beer—or whatever beverage you prefer. Do so whenever you like, but when you have a new client, there is still a *lot* of work to be done. Now you're moving into the *nurturing* phase of the business relationship.

If you haven't discovered this already, you will soon find how easy it is for a client to fall off the edge of the world and disappear if you allow it. If you need a refresher, a lot of the same skills involved in "following up" with a prospect from chapter 2 still apply here. But without maintaining the connection, it's very difficult to nurture your business relationships.

Even if it's just a quick check-in to make sure all is well, a "temperature check" is never a bad action. One method, especially with a client who isn't responding to you, is to attend seminars or conferences.

Some people feel like these are a waste of time because of the time spent away from the office, but it's still an opportunity. I have spent a lot of resources going to countless trade shows and seminars with the sole purpose of nurturing existing clients while simultaneously creating opportunities to form brand-new connections.

I've even used trade shows, conferences, and seminars as a place to reconnect with an ex-client who wanted nothing to do with me or my company. These are golden opportunities to set yourself up to obtain the intel you need to get a foot back in the door, especially if you have a difficult gatekeeper blocking you. Yet, by attending events like this, you are not setting your client or yourself up for judgment by anyone else in the organization, including the gatekeeper.

You have to be just as worried about *their* careers as your own career. Is there any risk for them in reconnecting with you?

I still have to give a word of caution here, and I advise using your best judgment in these kinds of situations. I once had a scenario where I needed to try to save the business relationship. So when I knew a big seminar was coming up, I looked for the big players' names within the disgruntled company to see if they were attending or even speaking at the event.

Sure enough, I found a couple of names I recognized from the organization, so off I went. At the conference, I was able to professionally rectify the issue they had with my company and build positive momentum toward resolution. The meeting wasn't forced, and in my mind, it was completely risk-free. After all, I was attending the seminar just like they were. They were not my only reason to attend, but I took the extra step to connect with them. More on "second chances" in the next section.

With trade shows and events, you have to remember how easy it can be to get comfortable behind a booth and hope potential opportunities walk up to you. Some will, but that's Sales Farming, not Sales Hunting. What if there is a golden boulder out in the crowd on the opposite end of the venue who doesn't even know you exist? How are you going to track them down if you're stuck behind a booth?

Instead, suit up and show up.

At the start of the book, I said a hunter is always moving, always learning, and always adapting. Bring this mindset to events too, whether it be to find a new client or to maintain and nurture the relationships of established clients. *Seek* them out. Don't allow the booth or your own desk to be a barrier.

Get out, move, and talk to *everyone*, because you never know what opportunity might open—or what information will clue you in to find your next piece of treasure.

Seriously, I have learned priceless information by simply showing up at some events and *observing*. One time, I recognized a client of mine across the room. As I approached, I noticed there was a queue of other people waiting to talk to him. Before this, I had no idea he was so highly regarded in the industry.

Walking up to him felt like the scene from *The Godfather* where everyone is lined up to kiss Don Corleone's ring and shake his hand. No joke, it was just like that.

I sat there in awe for about a half hour as more big-time decision-makers made sure my client knew they were there. To say it was eye-opening would be an understatement. Now I knew what a bigshot he was, I could pick up multiple clients simply by name-dropping my client. My brand gained credibility because I could say, "Yeah, I'm working with him."

Keep in mind, though, if you *do* name-drop an important client to gain a new one, just remember it's not only your reputation on the line but also your existing customer's reputation. You better be ready to bring your A-game if you are going to drop names. If you don't, that's the fast-track way to ruin your brand—and lose a client in the same breath.

When you attend any kind of event, have a plan of attack. Are you there to nurture relationships, gain new ones, or both? Who are you going to look for? Don't waste money and time by just attending to attend. Research the speakers ahead of time, look at the sponsors for the event, find out if your competitors will be there, make a list of breakout sessions or special events you want to go to, use your network to discover who you need an introduction to. All of these are easy actions you can take to stock up on your ammunition.

Or to go back to our treasure hunting analogy, treat the event like an open field of opportunity filled with giant rocks just waiting to be overturned. Who knows what you may learn, gain, and discover by simply suiting up and showing up?

A SECOND CHANCE

The road in sales can be bumpy and unpredictable. I mentioned earlier how mistakes will happen, rejection will happen, and failure will happen. It's all part of the job, but it doesn't mean there is no hope of redemption when a customer or prospect has parted ways with you and your company.

If you find yourself "fired" from an account, it's almost always a decision made by the company because of circumstances *outside* of your control. But if you *were* part of the problem and made a costly mistake that sent things south, all you can do is apologize and promise to make things right, no matter what it takes.

Taking ownership is not always easy to do, but your apology must be sincere and you need to only make it *once*. You'd be surprised how often a simple and sincere apology is all it takes to bring a customer back into the fold. Groveling or repeatedly apologizing is agony for everyone and will accomplish nothing more. There is no need to keep revisiting the mistake that caused the divide in the first place. If you reopen old wounds, they only get infected.

I get it. Sometimes in our zeal to apologize for errors we've committed or been involved in, we can end up apologizing multiple times for the same mistake to the same person. I have a firm belief that after the first apology, all subsequent apologies for the same incident will only fall on deaf ears. Instead, show you're worthy of their forgiveness by *solving* the problem. You never want clients to think your apologies are a way of deflecting blame.

There is another side to this coin, though. Sometimes if you are "fired" from an account, it isn't always negative. Don't let your pride dictate your actions. Yes, it stings when you lose an account, but maybe the client's expectations were unmeetable in the first place—or maybe they were just a bad customer.

Not all clients are going to be A+ clients.

Believe it or not, it doesn't matter how much those bad clients will spend if working with them is going to cause you and your team nothing but headaches. There are better options out there you could be spending your time on.

If you can keep your mindset positive, there's always something you can learn—whether or not you land an account. Sometimes the lesson learned is, "Yikes—I won't do that next time!" Even painful wins are still wins.

Instead of dwelling on the shots you've missed, refocus on how it will improve your aim next time around. You won't find the prized buck by thinking about what you're going to do *after* the hunting trip. You won't see their tracks in the dirt if you're looking in all the wrong places.

Where does the deer want to go?

Sales Hunters need to ask the same questions of their clients *and* prospects. Where do they want to go? What do they need in order to survive their specific industry? Once you know where they are headed and what they need, are you prepared to provide?

Don't be the Sales Hunter who forgot to bring enough ammunition. Come prepared and "stocked up" so when the time comes to pull the trigger on a deal, no booths, barriers, or objections can stand in your way.

CHAPTER 5

OVERCOMING OBJECTIONS

When I was eighteen, I started a new job as a lifeguard at the community pool. I had just graduated from high school on Thursday and the following Saturday was my first shift. I was excited for this new phase of my life, ready to soak up the sun *and* get paid at the same time.

Only fifteen minutes into my first shift, I had to dive to the bottom of the pool to pull out a drowning nine-year-old girl. I didn't have time to think, only react. Once I brought her to the surface, I realized she was unresponsive, so I started giving her mouth-to-mouth.

After a few adrenaline-filled seconds, she coughed up water and opened her eyes. I was just as shocked as she was. Shocked, but relieved! The paramedics arrived shortly after and took her to the hospital. But the main thing was she walked away from the pool that day with her life.

As incredible as it may sound, the lesson I learned that day wasn't from saving the little girl's life. It's what happened after.

I was so shaken by what had occurred, my whole body shivered as if I had just climbed out of a freezing lake in the middle of winter, not a city pool on a summer day. I felt like I was in a hazy dream, unsure if what just happened *actually* happened.

My manager took me into his office to help me calm down. He said, "You can do one of three things right now. One, you can stay in my office the rest of the afternoon, and if you don't step foot on the pool deck for the rest of your shift, that's fine. Two, you can stay in my office, take all the time you need, and then work the rest of your shift when you feel ready. Or three, you can go home for the rest of the day and come back tomorrow."

I had never wanted to go home so badly in my life. I wanted to scream at him, "Option three!" But all that came out was a feeble, "OK...."

Sensing my hesitation, he continued: "Before you decide, you should know the first two options are the best. If you decide to take option three and go home, I feel like I will never see you again, and I don't want that, Mike. You've already proven you can do the job we hired you for, and I don't want you to be afraid of it."

What he said resonated with me. You see, fear can keep you from doing what you want to do, what you're supposed to do. Fear is the strongest life repellent on the market. I don't know about you, but I never want to repel life. I want to live it. So...

I stayed.

I'm glad I did, too, because it taught me that even the most intense and difficult situations can be overcome with persistence. I will never forget that day for the rest of my life, and I still use it for motivation before an intimidating sales meeting or when trying to solve a difficult problem. No objection or rejection is too big to handle when we show persistence and simply never give up.

In a strange way, that adrenaline-filled shift taught me the greatest lesson imaginable for handling objections in my sales career. Objections are often just a wall of fear coming from a customer. Fear you can't actually solve their problem. Fear you aren't able to deliver on what you promise. Fear they'll regret the decision later on.

The objections you face will be very specific to your product and service—and to the needs of the client. In this chapter, I'm not going to pretend we can cover every possible scenario you'll encounter. Instead, I want to offer up some general counsel on cultivating a mindset that navigates you through the objection, regardless of the specific objection. Some objections will come up over and over. Others will appear once. They're just walls keeping you from closing the sale. So instead of focusing on the wall, let's focus on the ropes you need to climb over.

OVERCOMING THE WALL

Have you ever visited a car lot?

Imagine a man walks onto the lot filled with seemingly endless options of vehicles to choose from. He's excited but also a little stressed. But the cautious look on his face shows he wants to take it slow and just check out what the dealership has to offer. He plans on buying—after all, he wouldn't be there otherwise. But whether he's buying today—or from this lot—is up in the air.

Then—*Poof!* A salesman approaches from seemingly out of thin air. The customer didn't even hear him walk over. The salesman flashes a bright smile and asks, "Can I help you find anything?"

This is an innocent enough question. After all, it's clear the car-shopper is looking for *something*. But the car-shopper finds the salesman's approach jarring.

He sighs internally, avoids eye contact, and maybe grinds his teeth before replying, "No, I'm just looking."

The salesman has heard this same reply a million times, and every time he does, he wants to respond with something like: "Of course you're looking. You're at a car lot, for crying out loud! Are you familiar with every single car and the features they have? Are you aware of the current trends in the industry? Do you work at Auto Trader or something?"

Of course, this would not be the correct approach, right? This would only embarrass the customer and probably get the salesman in trouble with their boss. And there's nothing wrong with the question the salesman asked. After all, it's his job to help customers find what they're looking for.

But...

...when a salesperson *assumes* what a customer wants through nonverbal actions, it communicates to the prospect that you care more about yourself and your commission than their needs.

Let's take a deeper look at why the customer responded so negatively to a perfectly reasonable question. Why did "the wall" go up?

For starters, the customer was already unsure—they are just starting out in what can be a long and tedious process. Buying a car is a big decision. They don't want to be rushed. When the salesman approaches, they don't hear, "Can I help you?" They interpret this simple, innocent question as: "You better buy something from me right here, right now."

The customer's perception is, "You're just trying to get me to buy something today and I really don't want to deal with your pressure."

What could be an alternative approach?

Well, as salespeople, we still have to do our job and approach the customer. Otherwise we risk appearing rude, dismissive, or flat out lazy. But instead of asking the obvious first question that is guaranteed to put up "the wall," what if we asked, "So what brings you out to our car lot today?"

The underlying questions here are: "Why are YOU here? What problem do you need help solving? Are we the right people to help you solve that problem?"

The first question, "Can I help you?" is a "yes or no" question. You've got at least a 50 percent chance of getting a no.

The second question, "What brings you out today?" is open-ended. It doesn't assume but is a request for more information.

Unassuming questions are an invitation to an honest conversation. Questions like this can be asked during any kind of sales situation, not only in a car lot. During any sales meeting, before the prospect can even give you a "no," your first job isn't to sell—it's to figure out *why* they are even there. Why are they even giving you an opportunity to talk with them about the service or product you provide?

Have a conversation and see what happens. It might surprise you.

Your goal isn't to convince them you're right. It's to convince them *they* are right in making whatever decision they make. You might still get a "no," and that's OK. As I've said before, rejection is part of the job, and this job can be a roller-coaster of emotions.

Even when you get a "No," it's not the end of the story. In sales, the word "No" should be like breathing air. We need to see it as necessary for our survival, a cue to keep *hunting* for the next treasure.

YOUR GOAL ISN'T TO CONVINCE THEM YOU'RE RIGHT. IT'S TO CONVINCE THEM *THEY* ARE RIGHT IN MAKING WHATEVER DECISION THEY MAKE.

Use the power of "no" to your advantage. Remember, receiving a "No" is not indifference. Most of the time, "No" should be treated as an invitation to learn more.

Many times, a "No" is really the prospect telling you they still need to know "the why." Why should they buy from you and not your competitor? What can you do differently for them? They're not worried about your commission. They're worried about whether you can make their life easier. This means your real job is to help them understand *why* they should choose you and your company. Your job is to help them see you are invested in *their* future.

When you get a "No," it's a signal you're not going to close the deal right then, so you need to go back and find the pain points—and do more homework on the customer. In other words, you've got to *earn* the right to ask for their business. "No" means you haven't earned the right yet, so how will you go about earning it?

PAIN POINTS

Pain points don't sound like fun—and they aren't. But they are going to be a major reason an account stays with you during turbulent times—or they will be the reason they walk out the door. During the early phases of your relationship with a client, if you get a quick "yes" without discovering any of the customer's pain points, it's a big red flag. A red flag they will drop you as soon as the first pain point appears.

As nice as it is to close a deal and earn an "easy" commission, you might have to pump the brakes a bit and reassess the situation before going any further. If you discover the pain points first, you can either solve them or avoid them altogether. If you don't, then they will creep up and kill you down the road.

A while ago, my entire company was closed because of a holiday, but a customer reached out to me directly with an urgent need. Practicing what I preach, I took the call.

First lesson here: you have to realize a pain point will *never* come up when it's convenient. There's never a good time for it, period.

Now, I could've ignored the mess and dealt with it after the holiday. But I knew the mess would only get messier if I did so. Or I could dig into the mess right away and decipher what needed to be done to ensure the customer felt *cared* for. This doesn't mean you present a fireproof solution on the spot. Sometimes, it just means you acknowledge the issue and verbally commit to look into it.

In this instance, the customer was confused about a situation that had happened the day before and wanted clarification. With a little digging into the problem, not only did the customer have a solution by noon, but they were *thrilled* with the responsiveness I provided them on such short notice. All I had to do was make a few phone calls to clear up the lingering confusion.

Because I took a few hours on a holiday morning to address the pain point, how difficult do you think it will be for a competitor to come in and take away my account?

Very difficult.

Most pain points are not just one-off roadblocks, though. You could say the same about handling them. I've done this over and over again: Be responsive, show up, send a couple of quick emails, or take the time for a few phone calls (when no one else will), and there will *always* be a high reward attached to your efforts.

Maybe pain points are getting the best of you, though. Maybe you've heard a hundred "no's" and your existing accounts are all presenting pain points that make you feel like you're being buried alive.

What can you do when that happens?

LEAVE THE DAY

There will be plenty of days in sales that feel hopeless and direction-less. There will be plenty of clients who simply don't care how you feel either. Frankly, they've got their own feelings to worry about and it's not their job to carry yours. So the question is, how can you get back on track if you've steered off course and feel lost or unmotivated?

During my career, whenever I felt buried or unfocused, I've always seen it as my cue to leave the day behind and go do something else. Notice I said "leave the day," *not* "quit the day." I don't believe in quitting, but I do believe in finding another space outside of the office to breathe and gain perspective.

So what do I mean by leaving the day?

Well, it could be anything. For me, it could be going on a hike to clear my head, practice some self-reflection, or do whatever else it takes to find stable ground in my mind. Because if I'm feeling buried and stressed about a situation at work, I am only doing my team and myself a disservice by staying there. Without knowing it, I could exacerbate the issue even more—especially when dealing with a needy client who demands answers, not excuses. But if your wire is already thin, then the little problems you usually brush off could end up igniting the fuse and blow the whole thing up.

THE FASTER YOU GET BACK TO A GOOD HEADSPACE, THE FASTER YOU CAN GET BACK TO SOLVING THE PROBLEM WITH A PLAN—NOT PANIC.

Don't think that you'll break through if you just put your head down and grind harder. It won't happen! Especially on the days you're already stretched thin. Instead, go out and remind yourself of the rewards this job can offer. The faster you get back to a good headspace, the faster you can get back to solving the problem with a plan—not panic.

Sometimes the best way to leave the day is to go buy something.

Seriously. Retail therapy can be just what the doctor ordered! Obviously, I don't mean you should go overboard and buy a new car you can't afford, but a simple self-care purchase can snap you out of a funk.

Maybe you have a close friend, life coach, or family member you can reach out to and talk through the difficult situation together. Find someone who can offer a fresh perspective to you. Just make sure those you seek advice from are worthy of giving advice. Otherwise, it's like going to the doctor and asking about your tooth pain. They might help your pain a little, but you'd need to go to the dentist for an accurate examination, right?

Seek advice from people who can check all three of these essential boxes:

People with the right skills and know-how

People you trust

People you like

In other words, you're not getting advice from the lowest producer on the team who has nothing but complaints to offer. And you're not getting advice from the person you think would swoop in and steal the client from you when they hear about the problem you're having. I know this sounds obvious, but the source of the advice often determines whether it's actually worth following.

You may even have a client who has become a good friend. You'll have your share of tough clients, but you'll also discover some incredible people and make lifelong friends in the process. If you have a client who's a friend, remember to keep the personal stuff separate from work stuff. They are your client first and friend second. I'm not saying you don't ever talk to them about your personal life but keep the business talk separate as much as possible.

For example, here's a couple "what to do" versus "what NOT to do" scenarios:

WHAT TO DO (BUSINESS CONVERSATION)

"I have a client with Such-and-Such Problem who is threatening to cancel their account with us. I've tried X, Y, and Z and they've rejected all these options. I value your input, so do you think there's something I might be overlooking still?"

WHAT NOT TO DO (BUSINESS CONVERSATION)

"I have a client with Such-and-Such Problem who is threatening to cancel their account with us. If I lose them, I'm going to lose my job, my house, my truck, and my dog. You've gotta help me out!"

WHAT TO DO (PERSONAL CONVERSATION)

"I could really use a vacation. Where would you recommend?"

WHAT NOT TO DO (PERSONAL CONVERSATION)

"I could really use a vacation. Think you can talk your boss into increasing our order? The extra commission would really help me out."

I know these are a bit of an exaggeration, but I think you get the point. It's a hard balance to strike, but if you find a happy medium with a client, then a career in sales can be fulfilling in other areas outside of making money.

A piece of advice I personally like to follow is to stay away from the bar—especially with a client. Bars tend to brew harmful situations waiting to happen. The goal of leaving the day is not to *forget* the hard stuff, but to step away to regain clarity, so that when you are ready, you come back even stronger.

Instead of the bar, go bowling, go watch a movie, go do a workout, or go walk your dog. There are literally a million other things you can do. If you want to be successful, you have to be on your A+ game. If you aren't on your A+ game, how do you expect to land A+ accounts?

I was watching a pro football game recently where a wide receiver had several intense plays in a row. I watched as he ran full speed, cut to his left on a dime, and leapt four feet into the air to catch the ball. It was no wonder when he called to the sidelines for a breather.

Likewise, to bring your A+ game—to run the routes at full speed—you have to let yourself catch your breath sometimes. If you're too sore or too exhausted to overcome your competition, you will be no good when it matters most.

Simply put, leaving the day means doing whatever it takes to return to full strength. This way, when an opportunity comes to the table, you're not winded but ready to negotiate the deal of a lifetime.

NEGOTIATION

It's no surprise that negotiation is a major part of sales. The word itself conjures up pictures of important-looking businesspeople with big titles, wearing fancy suits and serious faces, sitting around a massive oak table with a stack of documents before them. While sometimes it *can* look like this, the one thing for certain is that negotiation is a vital skill for the salesperson to cultivate.

One tool we must have in our kit is the ability to negotiate a deal that works best for all parties involved. No one should ever enter the negotiation phase without a clear understanding of the goal and purpose that needs to be accomplished. Otherwise, it's like asking a receiver to run a route he doesn't know. It probably won't end well.

In addition to having a clear outline of what you want to achieve through the process of negotiation, you also need to have a priority list of the issues most relevant to achieving your desired end. You don't want to create your own impediments before the negotiation even begins. Plus, when you compromise on an issue, you're going to need to be able to explain the reason for the compromise.

The toughest part for the sales professional is we truly have to keep *both* parties in mind the entire time. We *are* the middleman. On one side, we represent our prospect/client's needs. At the same time, we represent our company's needs. This sounds impossible when you first think about it.

I imagine this like I am on a seesaw with myself—trying to balance without letting my feet hit the ground. I want to give the client what they want, but I know I can't give *too* much or more than what the company is willing to give. Up and down, up and down. But just like playing on a seesaw, you can make this process fun if you choose!

Many people refer to negotiation as striving to get the win/win scenario. I, on the other hand, believe this is nearly impossible to achieve. Both sides are looking for a positive outcome and give little regard to the goals of the other side. To truly represent the goals of any organization during a negotiation, you need to be focused on their needs. This seems easy enough on the surface, but for you as the salesperson, it means your focus needs to be split on the needs and goals of *both* sides.

I've found the best way to achieve balance on the seesaw is surprisingly simple: I choose to be pro-client in front of the company and pro-company in front of the client.

Here's the deal: If you draw hard dividing lines in the sand, *no one* is going to be happy with the result. No one gets to where they want to be and guess who *both* parties are going to blame for the deadlock?

That's right, *you*.

You are the wilderness guide here. If you have no sense of direction, no map,

> **I CHOOSE TO BE PRO-CLIENT IN FRONT OF THE COMPANY AND PRO-COMPANY IN FRONT OF THE CLIENT.**

and no compass, then the negotiation will trail off into the middle of nowhere.

Imagine a scenario here. Let's say a client asks you to cut prices by 50 percent but you already know your company has cut the price by 20 percent with a 30 percent margin built in to produce a 10 percent profit. This means you have a fairly confident hunch your company will scoff at their steep request.

Don't shut the client down just because you think the margin is getting too thin. If you don't at least take the offer back to your employer, are you negotiating on behalf of the company—or yourself?

Always listen to what the requests are, whether they're realistic or not—then take it back to the company either way. Now, my caveat here is sometimes requests are *so* unrealistic they don't deserve to see the light of day. They are rare and extreme, but they can happen. For example, if somebody asked me to do something illegal, there would be no need to discuss it further with the other party. It's critical to maintain ethical business relationships, *especially* when it comes to negotiation.

Negotiation is really no different from handling any objection you encounter. As I see it, you need to come to a solid understanding of the goals and needs of the other side to get the best possible outcome for *all* sides. Once you have a clear map of the goals for both your company and the client, you can use open-ended questions, probing questions, and observations to discover where the potential middle ground is.

For instance, don't be afraid to ask about your prospect's previous provider or your competition. Ask a probing question like, "What has your current/previous provider done *right*?" After listening, you can then add to their response with what you will bring to the table that's better. So if they answer, "Well, our current provider is great at taking our calls right away," then your response is, "I'll take your calls AND respond to your emails." There's a lot of advantage in knowing the potential wins and objections based on their previous experiences.

Zig Ziglar said it best, "When you throw dirt at people, you're not doing a thing but losing ground."[4] Your goal is to gain ground. Learning what your competition did right only helps you here. Another subtle reason for asking about your competition is acknowledging your prospect's intelligence. Make them notice their good business sense for originally picking your competitor. No one wants to hear they made a bad business decision—even if it's the truth. But now you have the opportunity to *match* what your competitor did right—*and* rise above it.

The key in all of this is listening. There are aspects about your service you know are beneficial, but you still have to listen to what the

---

4   Zig Ziglar, "Losing Ground," Ziglar.com, accessed March 24, 2023, https://www. ziglar.com/quotes/when-you-throw-dirt-at-people/.

customer actually wants first. Listen to what your prospect has to say and *how* they say it. In the early stages of negotiating, they may not let you know exactly what they want to achieve, but if you pay attention to the items they identify as important to them—or not important to them—they will give you insight concerning where they want to go. No one tells you what they want at the *end* of a negotiation. If you haven't discovered their needs until the end, then you've missed your opportunity and a deal/solution is probably not going to happen.

Assume nothing. Hunt for the right question. You don't need to be the smartest guy in the room during a negotiation. If you try to make yourself the smartest guy, then I have some humbling news for you: you're *not*. People who believe they're the best or smartest can easily overlook the essential details needed to ensure a successful negotiation.

A good approach to have is a "tell me more" attitude compared to rushing for answers. With the "tell me more" approach, you won't find yourself cornered. You will actually have more leeway to pause and *not* have an answer right away. You can confidently respond, "Let me check into that and I will get back to you," so you can bring the question back to your company and brainstorm the best solution.

This approach gives you a chance to walk away, take a breather, and come back with a sound answer that benefits everyone in the long run. You don't want to be the end-all, be-all, tell-all. It's to your advantage during a negotiation to *not* give an answer as soon as you think you have one. It's better to say, "I think I know a way to solve this, but you know what? I want to check with a couple of other people to make sure it's the best answer." Being a Sales Hunter isn't just about hunting prospects—it's also about hunting the right solutions.

MEETING IN THE MIDDLE

When you relay the information you received during the negotiation back to your company—whether it's good or bad—always filter it through the lens of knowing your company does not want to give anything up. They want to be the outright winners of the deal, right?

For instance, I never start any conversation with the end goal in sight. There is always room for give and take in every conversation, even with your employer. Remember, just because you left your client or prospect at the table, it doesn't mean the negotiation has ended. It has only entered the next phase because now you are negotiating with your employer on your prospect/client's behalf. It can be a weird position to find yourself, but such is the life of the middleman.

First and foremost, just like how you need a road map of where the conversation is going with the client, you need the same with your employer. What exactly are you going to relay to your company? Pick out the most important elements from the conversations with the prospect that you KNOW your employer needs to hear.

For example, let's say the prospect wants the pricing to be adjusted. Well, in some industries, especially in California, you can get in big trouble for violating rates. So if the prospect is questioning the rates I offer, I can't take that information back to the company. If I did, it would be a gigantic waste of everyone's time, including the prospect's.

But this isn't the case for most people in sales. Pricing is about *perceived* value. It's the difference between Nordstrom and Walmart. Who doesn't want the best price when purchasing a service or product?

For me, if pricing is the main issue I take away from the negotiation, my company won't need to tell me what I need to do next. I already know I have to go back and reestablish *value* in some other way. I have to find alternatives I can bring to the table and demonstrate, "This is what you're getting at our prices and why we charge this rate. Here's what *you* get out of it, how it's the best deal for *you*."

Now, there are situations where the company makes a mistake and the client demands compensation. This is a very different type of negotiation. I found myself in a situation just like this, which I mentioned briefly earlier on. The client was upset and demanded a multimillion dollar settlement. As for my company, they wanted to settle for much less. So the negotiation started with a severe divide between both sides. No one was happy.

From a legal standpoint, my company was on pretty solid ground. But my priority was to save the relationship, not win an argument. If the disagreement went to court, then the business relationship would be forever fractured. So I had to define what the relationship was worth, and I committed to management that I would service the account to bring in more business after the dust settled.

The process was long and tedious, but I kept going back and forth, representing both the client and my company. Finally, we struck the middle ground—we found the balance in the seesaw. Both sides were still not as happy as they *wanted* to be, but to me, that's a great sign a truly fair deal is struck. Everyone agreed upon the terms and it was settled.

EVERYONE HAS TO FEEL A BIT OF PAIN IN A COMPROMISE.

Going into the negotiation, everyone wants a win, but that simply does not happen. Everyone has to feel a bit of pain in a compromise.

But at least the pain is shared, making it bearable. Everybody has to give something to get something. The only way you can meet in the middle is if everyone agrees to budge some on what they really want. In this case, what we really wanted was to continue working together after the settlement. Even as I write this, I am still doing all of the business with this client.

TOUGH LOVE

How do we keep ourselves emotionally fit to handle the day-to-day issues that arise? We can't leave the day as soon as the first objection comes our way. That's why it's so important to surround yourself with someone who looks at problems from a different angle than you do.

We need people around us who have a unique set of thoughts and beliefs, people who are bold enough to challenge our thought process when it needs to be questioned. You need people who will show you the "tough love" necessary to avoid comfortability with the status quo.

I have several of those people in my life, and every time I decide to look at the world through rose-colored glasses, they step up and remind me of the truth.

These are the people who will encourage you and help you keep moving in the right direction. These are the people who make you successful, the ones you need on your team for life.

When I first started working in the mortgage business, I worked for ninety days straight. Weekends and holidays didn't matter to me. I was determined to generate revenue as quickly as possible. I created scenarios to motivate myself to keep pushing for the deal, and because of this, I created a lot of pressure that spilled over onto the operational staff.

One day, my manager pulled me aside and said, "Mike, we are getting some complaints about how you're working."

I wasn't sure what he meant. I was so laser-focused on my goals, I replied, "I'm just trying to bring revenue in!"

He continued: "Yes, but on each one of those deals you bring in, how much do you get paid?"

The question made little sense at first. "You know what I get paid for each sale."

He then asked, "How much do you think *they* get paid?" By *they*, he was referring to the support and operational staff.

"I have no idea what they earn," I admitted with a shrug.

"Exactly," he nodded. "So do you think they have the same motivation as you?"

"No," I said. Suddenly I saw how I was putting *my* desires, motivation, and expectations squarely on the shoulders of the people I needed to reach my goals.

"Your sales job doesn't end outside the office," he continued. "It comes inside the office too. Your goal is to fill up *your* checkbook, but that's not the staff's goal. So find a way to get them to do what you want them to do without beating them up. If you keep this up, you won't meet your goals."

That conversation changed the way I looked at this job. I learned the importance of tough love and how sales never stops.

Remember, everyone's in sales! I'm selling the company on why I'm doing the business, I'm selling the client on why they are doing business with me, and I'm selling the operational staff on why they need to be working on my deal. Of course, management needs to be sold on the fact the deal is a good business match for the company, too.

If my math is accurate, that makes four different "clients" I have to focus on during each sale. All of them are critical to my success and all of them bring unique objections to my doorstep.

You need clients in front of you *and* people backing you up.

I'm not the smartest guy in the room, but that's OK. I surround myself with smart people. Sales is impossible if you try the lone-wolf approach.

FINISH THE SHIFT

When I think back to my first shift at the community pool, all the emotions come swirling back as if I was still sitting in my manager's office, trying to process saving the little girl's life. I'm sure to some people, finishing the shift wouldn't be important, but to me it was. It wasn't about showing how tough I was or how good of a worker I was. I had nothing more to prove as a lifeguard that day.

The reason I needed to finish that shift was about overcoming my *own* objection, my *own* wall, and negotiating with *my* feelings of fear, and then accepting the tough love and advice from someone I trusted.

Sometimes finishing the shift is all we can do. Every day will bring a new objection, a new barrier for you to overcome. It's not one you can bulldoze through by putting your head down and gritting your teeth. Instead of potentially hurting yourself more, embrace the moment or lesson being offered to you. That wall might not be as scary as you thought and instead of knocking it down, you might just be able to walk *through* it, if you only stop first to take a look.

DESTROYING THE OBJECTION ISN'T THE SAME AS ADDRESSING IT!

Overcoming objections is never just about a price point or a feature. They may be factors, but they're usually just walls concealing the pain point on the other side. You can answer an objection and still lose the deal. Why? Because destroying the objection isn't the same as addressing it! Maybe you didn't understand your prospect's pain points or how to negotiate through them. Maybe you didn't know how to treat yourself or the support team working with you. But if you can keep these keys in hand, they will unlock any door within any wall, allowing you to build your sales business the way you want.

CHAPTER 6

BUILDING YOUR SALES BUSINESS

Starting and owning your own business is considered by some to be the American Dream. The thought itself is inspiring for many: breaking free from the rat race, from corporate greed, and, most importantly, being your own boss.

What many people don't realize is just how much money, time, and resources are needed to succeed. The idea for a business is only a small part of the equation. After a long, stressful battle to launch, many new businesses get buried in debt and fade away. I've seen signage for a new business go from "Grand Opening" to "Liquidation Sale" within six months.

One thing's for sure: building a business is tough.

For those of us in sales, though, we are in a fascinating position. Like an entrepreneur, we are driven by a desire to obtain the greatest market share possible. Successful Sales Hunters build their sales businesses as if they are running their own businesses.

In a lot of ways, we *are* running our own businesses. As a reminder, the only real difference in how a sales professional works compared to a business owner is that salespeople don't have any overhead costs weighing them down. In many ways, we have more freedom than a small business owner.

How so?

The small business owner has to feed the company, even in success. With sales, the company feeds *you*.

Knowing this, if you treat your sales position as if you are running your own business, you will reap the rewards for your hard work. If you can approach it with the same drive, ownership, and level of commitment as an entrepreneur, then you stand a real chance to succeed. Sure, you have to share the profits with the company you work for, but most commissions are a lot better than any normal salary I've seen.

So the million-dollar question is, "How do we build our sales business to succeed?"

We build our business with an entrepreneurial mindset focused on the future while paying attention to the current marketplace at all times. That's exactly what I did when I started my notary business I mentioned before.

You might recall the secret of my success was I simply paid attention to the general marketplace of real estate. I noticed there was a propensity to hand off the final step during the home purchasing process—the document signing—to an external individual for the notarization. Looking at the bare minimum requirements, I wondered, "What would it take for someone to hire me as the notary instead?"

After doing research, I picked a specific niche to service in closing new construction home loans. From there, I formed my business around how I could differentiate myself within this already specific niche. You see, it's all about the details within the details. It's all about where you can make yourself the expert voice.

For example, athletic shoes aren't a new market. So don't be the person who just sells athletic shoes. Be the person who knows the best shoes for point guards to wear. Don't be the person who just sells mobile phones. Be the person who knows the best mobile phone for teachers to use. That's the power of finding your niche.

Even though home building was already a specific marketplace, I still had competition. There were other notaries more established than I was. So the next question I had to ask myself was: "How can I set myself apart from the competition?"

I took inventory of my experience through exploratory questions: What do I do best? More importantly, what do I *know* best?

The more I thought about it, the more I realized I had vast experience in every other aspect of the real estate transaction process. So much so, I started selling my expertise in the marketplace. I wasn't just your dime-a-dozen notary—I became a one-person signing process. I could answer a wide variety of questions raised by the buyer (or buyers) about the process, freeing the escrow officer to allocate their precious time to other aspects of the deal. By hiring me for my expertise, they could simplify their lives. My sales pitch was basic: "Just hire me and I can help you with everything you need."

I firmly established the "why" for me, but the "why" for home buyers didn't seem quite right to succeed long term. So I kept digging, kept searching for the treasure within my own business structure, and really looked at the whole home-buying process.

Even if you think you know everything about your market, look again. Remember, treasures don't sit on the surface.

When I looked again, I learned the only time a buyer sits down with any representative to talk about escrow (apart from their real estate agent) was during the closing process. Someone in my position was literally the one person a buyer would sit down with for over an hour to decide whether they should sign their life away on the biggest purchase they will probably ever make.

Talk about a big deal!

After talking through my thought process with the escrow office, they understood the advantage in having me handle the issues arising during the entire escrow process. I could explain everything to the buyer, help them truly understand all the complex paperwork. I made people actually read the documents. In fact, I made *myself* read the documents of the loan package—I couldn't justify asking someone to sign a document I myself hadn't read. My purpose—and my value—was to make sure the entire process wasn't a headache for the escrow office or the buyer by ensuring we were all *literally* on the same page.

So when the client went home, and their family and friends asked them how the closing went, instead of them saying the usual, "It was pretty mind-numbing and I just wanted to be done with it," my goal was for them to be able to smile and say, "It was actually pretty easy and enlightening thanks to Mike."

I took this same concept with me when I went to work later on for a Fortune 500 company. In fact, my little notary business was the exact reason they wanted me. Once I started, I created a team of notaries, recorded training videos for them, and made sure when the time came we could offer those same services to our customers.

As a hunter, you may never even see a 20-point buck for years, but the more prevalent 8-point and 10-pointers will prepare you for the day the big buck decides to show up. In other words, the entrepreneurial mindset from my notary business opened doors and prepared me for bigger opportunities down the road. That's why it matters now what you do with your sales business. You never know what's next.

TAKING SELF-INVENTORY

Since building your own sales business as a Sales Hunter requires much of the same mindset and energy as an entrepreneur, let's go a little deeper. What does taking a self-inventory look like for the average professional salesperson?

Think of it like this: If a company has taken the time and resources to train and equip you with the tools needed to succeed within their system, why wouldn't you do the same for yourself? Why not figure out what *you* do faster, cheaper, and better than everyone else?

What do you want to be known for?

When I first started in sales, I looked around the office and noticed we were all trying to sell the same piece of paper. That is, we all had the same rate sheet with an interest rate typed on it. I know that's oversimplifying my job a bit, but it's true. I thought, "If we are all selling the same thing, the same way, on the same day, how can I be different?"

Taking self-inventory is about finding how *you* can be different.

Take a look inside of yourself and see what you find. Leave the day behind! Go do whatever you need to do to unwind, not for the sake of blowing off some steam, but to find what makes *you* unique! Then make a list and narrow it down to

MYSTERY IS WHERE MISUNDERSTANDING CAN HAPPEN.

what makes the most sense for you and your career. Envision how you want to be known throughout the industry. When people hear your name, what's going to be the first word they associate with it?

For me, I focused on building my reputation by being *honest.* I was going to tell my clients the truth—and not only when it benefited me, but ALWAYS. I'd rather tell someone what I'm doing and they be dissatisfied than it be a mystery. Mystery is where misunderstanding can happen. It's why I'm so quick to say "no"—I don't want to disappoint a client later and then it becomes a bigger issue than it needs to be. I want to be proactive in helping them find a solution to their problems in ways my company can contribute. If that's not possible, then I want them to understand from the beginning what our limitations are. On those rare occasions when we do not fit their needs, I'm not delaying them in accomplishing their company goals, which increases their perception of me as an honest ally.

SHOW ... DON'T TELL

Being honest will always be the correct thing to do in sales—and life, in general. But being honest isn't just about what you say—it's about what you *do* and *how* you do it. So when you have your list made, just know those are still only words. You know the old saying "actions speak louder than words"?

Well, it's the truth. If you want to set yourself apart from the crowd, you have to follow through with action.

You can tell someone how great you are all day long, but that is never the differentiator when closing a deal or building your sales business. The more you *tell* someone what you are, the less they *believe* who you are. But if you *demonstrate* who you are, it speaks louder than anything else you could say. Nothing will ever make a bigger statement about your character than how you act. In the long run, how you put the words from your self-inventory list into action will either make you or break you.

I recently had some work done in my house. The company I contracted to do the work tossed cement in my trashcan. Not a great idea since cement dries and eventually hardens, making my trashcan useless. Strike one.

The company didn't tell me about it either. Instead, they created a mystery for me to stumble across. I learned what had happened after the trash wasn't picked up on trash day. Strike two.

I called up the owner of the construction company and told him about the situation. Without hesitation, he came out to my house, was very apologetic, and fixed the problem. Instead of striking out with me, he hit a home run with how quickly he solved the issue. He could've just apologized over the phone by making a nice word salad for me. Instead, he

USE YOUR WORDS TO SET THE BAR. USE ACTION TO FOLLOW THROUGH.

took action and backed up his apology by actually fixing the problem.

Everyone makes mistakes. But don't let your sales business suffer because of them. Apologies have no truth in them if there is no action behind them. This is a major part of building your reputation, which we will talk about more in the next chapter. But for now, remember this: Use your words to set the bar. Use action to follow through.

The result will be steady growth and a loyal customer base who trusts you because you've shown them you are a person *of* your word, not a person *full* of words.

The best part is after you've steadily put your words into action, your competition will have to change their methods to try to get over the bar *you* set. I don't know about you, but I like to set the bar. When you are the one setting the bar, you dictate what success looks like. You choose what it means to you. Because that's all any of this is, right? A choice to find the treasure wherever you are, a choice to succeed. Nothing about this is revolutionary. It's just basic stuff anyone can do if they choose. Say what you do, do what you say. In that exact order.

CONTROLLING YOUR FUTURE

Without having a business-building mindset in sales, it's easy to get complacent or even bored. After all, you go to work for company X every day, selling product Y to the consumer. Your name isn't on the company letterhead. You don't have millions of dollars invested in the company either. So why the heck should you care?

Well, if you're like most sales professionals, money is the ultimate motivator. Let's just be honest about it. And how do you make more money in sales? You sell more.

> But how *much* money could you make selling product Y? Well, that's actually your choice. This is both the beauty and the beast in sales.

Having a business-building mindset in sales naturally gives you a sense of ownership, which generates motivation and drive.

Once I developed a skill set and knew *how* to sell, the product I was selling didn't matter. Skills can transfer into any market or product—I just happened to find a product I liked and built a business off of it. This didn't happen overnight, though.

Even with all the position changes I made in the industry, I was still building my business the entire time. From real estate sales to mortgage sales to title sales, I covered it all. The reason I was successful was that it was all *mine*. I wasn't technically the owner of the building, but I had an owner's mindset. I realized my brand, my reputation, and my business came down to my desire to be in control of my future.

You can't control your own future if you're waiting for your company to feed validation to you. Don't let external validation drive your bus. Take control of the steering wheel yourself. This way, even if you switch companies and the name on the side of the "bus" changes, it won't matter. Who you get paid by shouldn't change your business-building mindset.

In fact, you can take ownership by negotiating your salary based on *your* needs. The company is not the one driving the bus. You are.

Pop quiz time: Once you are logistically satisfied, what's the difference between you and the guy in the corner market making and selling widgets?

You don't have any ugly overhead costs!

You don't have to worry about rent. That's the company's problem. You don't have to worry about buying the product. That's the company's problem. You have an entire list of expenses that *aren't* your problem! That's not the case when it's your name on the building.

YOU WANT TO OWN YOUR BUSINESS, NOT BE OWNED BY THE BUSINESS.

For example, I get to expense all the miles I drive my car for business-related matters. Well, that's a lot of miles, meaning more money in my pocket when tax season comes along. Most companies will even pay for you to attend conferences or seminars, and if you remember from chapter 4, events like this are *great* places to hunt prospects, build your brand, close deals, and nurture relationships. So your company is paying you to make *more* money for yourself!

You are free to function *as* an entrepreneur without the worries and expenses that can bog you down. All you have to worry about is building relationships, establishing your own brand, and then collecting your commission. Notice those are all aspects of the job where you have some element of control.

You want to own your business, not be owned by the business. If you're not looking at your sales position in this way, then you are just an employee who gets a salary. If you take ownership, you have the greatest say about what your value is to the company.

TAKING OWNERSHIP MEANS TAKING CONTROL OF YOUR IDENTITY—WHAT YOU WANT TO BE KNOWN FOR.

Just like clients, employers will come and go, but you are always going to be you. At the end of the day, that's what really matters. Taking ownership means taking control of your identity—what you want to be known for.

KEEP YOUR PROMISES

When it comes to building your sales business, the process really boils down to the service you provide your clients. Again, this isn't rocket science, just common sense.

You see, a client doesn't care about anyone else's issues. Their whole focus is on resolving the issues *they* have. The only way to ensure your client does not pick up the phone and call your competition is by making sure they understand you will always get back to them when they call.

No day is ever over until every call has received a response on the same day they called you. Even if this means informing your client you are on the problem but need a little more time to research the potential solutions. No one likes to feel ignored and most clients will give you the time you need for a great solution if you just acknowledge their request.

I once took an after-hours call that ended with me getting an account I had been grooming for five long years. Why? Because they were not getting follow-up from my competition. The interesting part is the client had insisted to me for those five years that my competition's follow-up would never fail them.

To avoid having a hard conversation with the client, their existing service provider vanished without a word. Their failure to communicate became my golden opportunity. My simple promise to the client was, "If you ever call me, I will always get back to you as soon as humanly possible." Fortunately, they gave me a chance to keep this promise. Essentially, they said to me, "Mike, you said you'd follow up. Now prove it." So I did.

Mystery and doubt create the perception you are not focused on their business. All you need to do to change the perception is to let your client know you are getting the right people involved and working out a plan.

When tough situations arise, you know the ins and outs of your business and the limitations and strengths of those you work with. All that's left to do is prove the client made the right choice in trusting you. Once you build this level of trust with your clients, they're going to give you more of their problems to solve, which means more commission for you.

The biggest compliment I ever receive is when a client contacts me to see if my competition's solutions are within my guidelines—and then they give me the deal instead. No one wants to micromanage problems—they just want solutions focused on their needs and business model. They want to know their priority is also a priority for you—and that you handle it effectively and efficiently.

When you're a salesperson who keeps their promises, you will find there is no better or more rewarding way to make a quality living on your own terms.

A SALESPERSON VERSUS A GREAT SALESPERSON

I've been saying it all chapter, but your success in building a sales business comes from a choice within yourself. Will you just be a salesperson or will you be a *great* salesperson?

What does being a *great* salesperson look like, though?

It's a blend of everything we've talked about so far.

Will you keep your promises? Will you show your work and not just talk about it? Will you research and advise your clients accurately and on time? Will you choose to dig deeper even when it feels like you've hit the bottom of the earth?

A life in sales is a life of hard choices, hard decisions, and correcting mistakes. You're going to have to take bullets in front of your clients by saying, "I made a mistake and I will make it right." You can't lay blame on the people behind you, even when it *is* their fault. For one thing, once you throw someone under the bus, it's really hard to get them back on the bus when you need them there.

SHARE THE PRAISE, TAKE THE BLAME, AND DON'T THROW PEOPLE UNDER THE BUS.

But also, when you lay blame on the people working behind the scenes, a smart client is going to ask, "Why did you give my stuff to them if you knew they were bad at their job?" Now you have *two* problems to solve, not one.

Instead, share the praise, take the blame, and don't throw people under the bus. Most salespeople don't do this. Great salespeople take the time to catalog who makes them successful behind the scenes.

I always remain the visible, responsible party—taking the credit *and* blame—that's what I actually get paid for. I don't get paid to do a title report—I get paid to convince someone we're the right people to *do* the title report. If the client isn't getting what they expected, then it's my job to manage and fix what's happening. Don't allow mystery to creep into your business relationships. Stay available and honest no matter what.

That's what will separate you from the average everyday salesman and make you a great one.

YOUR CUSTOMER'S PERCEPTION MUST BE YOUR REALITY.

I'm going to say it again for the people in the back: *your customer's perception must be your reality.* Not only is this a vital piece in building your sales business, but it's what helps establish your reputation in the industry for years to come.

CHAPTER 7

OWNING YOUR REPUTATION

As much as hunters are on the move, there are also times to camp down. In my experience, this has been only when we knew, without a doubt, we were in an area animals like to pass through. Before camping down, we would have already spent hours tracking, clearing brush, hiking, and then preparing to win the hunt before we had even spotted any prey.

In the same way, your reputation helps prepare the way to "win" the sale without having a conversation.

If you haven't done so already, you'll soon discover your reputation has a voice. Did you ever realize there are meetings you attended without you being there in person? That's because even if you aren't in a room, your reputation *is*. Your reputation is present when you're absent, so you need to take every opportunity to make sure it's good!

> **YOUR REPUTATION IS PRESENT WHEN YOU'RE ABSENT.**

Always remember the power of perception. The perception of others must be your reality!

I don't know about you, but I want to be represented well when I'm not physically in the room. I want to be known as someone who *honors* his word. I learned this firsthand while working with the County of Riverside, California.

A farmer had been renting his land from the county for a while, but the county decided to renege on some of the previous commitments they had made. Lucky me, I was chosen by management to deliver the bad news we were about to break some promises. Talk about drawing the short straw...

While I was doing this, the farmer shared with me a thought I've never forgotten throughout my entire career. He asked, "Do you know why the good Lord never put bones in our tongues?"

"I have no idea," I replied.

The farmer continued, "He didn't put bones in our tongues so if we break our word to someone, we don't feel the pain we should. Instead, we feel the burden deep in our souls."

I understood exactly what he meant.

Even though it wasn't my fault, I felt the burden of the broken promise. I immediately wished I could've handled the situation in a different manner for him. Yet there was nothing else I could do or say.

At the same time, I learned a valuable lesson. I made a personal commitment to avoid breaking my own word, no matter the personal cost to me. My word was my brand and, therefore, my word was my reputation. Reputation is never just about what you say. It's always about *doing* what you say. It's about being a thermostat—setting the temperature—instead of being a thermometer who rises and falls based on external factors.

UNDERPROMISE AND OVERDELIVER

We are first and foremost human beings, and I have yet to meet a perfect one. I know I have stated this consistently already, but it's always worth repeating: you're going to make mistakes! There is no avoiding them, but how you *respond* is what will either strengthen your reputation or ruin it.

I want to expand a bit on a previous story I shared where my company made a mistake and had to pay out a large sum of money. After the dust settled, the client told me, "I expect this will *never* happen again."

I replied, "Well, I can't make that promise."

At first, the look on the client's face was a mix between shock and unease.

So I clarified, saying, "What I *can* promise you is we'll put measures in place to prevent this mistake from happening again."

Suddenly, the anxious look etched across my client's face relaxed. Think about what would've happened if I had promised I would never make another mistake! Even worse, what if I had promised I would never make the *same* mistake I just cleaned up when it had been completely outside of my control?

I would be setting myself up for failure.

My personal brand and reputation would instantly be on the line, and when the moment the next mistake happened, I would be at fault. Even if I had no control over a new mistake happening, I'd be responsible for breaking the promise I made.

If I am made out to be a liar and lose the client, who does it hurt the most? Sure, the company will hurt a little, but they are so big, the loss of one client will barely make a dent in the corporate bottom line. It's much more of a loss for me. The loss to me is 100 percent of their business!

The worst thing you can do is overpromise and underdeliver.

The best you can do is underpromise and overdeliver.

When you make your first impression, you set the bar. If you set the bar at ten feet in the air, you can't go below the bar and expect to be rewarded. You *can't* back down from the expectations you set yourself.

Imagine if a middle school pole vaulter sets the bar at World Record height. It's great for them to have a long-term goal to break the world record, but what are the realistic chances they can do so at the age of twelve? Not great. In other words, don't set the bar at a height you can't meet yet.

You don't want to be caught looking up in bewilderment when you have to meet your own expectations. Instead, set the bar in a place where you can always raise it higher with the more experience and success you achieve.

THE WORST THING YOU CAN DO IS OVERPROMISE AND UNDERDELIVER. THE BEST YOU CAN DO IS UNDERPROMISE AND OVERDELIVER.

Let's say you purchase a lawn mower with a five-year warranty. Two years later, the mower breaks. You call up the company to honor the warranty and they replace the faulty part. Afterward, the sales rep contacts you to ensure everything is working properly and you're still a happy customer.

So far, so good, right?

Well, after talking with the salesperson for a bit, they try to convince you the mower will never break again for the next five years. Would you believe them?

I wouldn't.

Not when it literally broke after two years of use! That's the whole reason for the warranty. The warranty isn't a promise "It won't ever break." Instead, it's a promise "If and when it breaks, here's what we'll do to make it right." So if the rep claimed it wouldn't break again, not only would I lose trust in the rep, but I'd question their product as well. The salesperson is setting up their company and themselves for a damaged reputation.

The only truthful promise you should make if you find yourself in a similar situation should sound like this: "No matter what happens, we will make it right."

NAVIGATING THE HORIZON

Like mistakes, change is unavoidable. Also like mistakes, how you navigate through sudden change will impact your reputation and your clients. Your job is to mitigate the impact a sudden change can have on your client and get them up to speed ASAP.

In a business relationship, your client is entrusting you to steer their figurative ship in the right direction. How foolish would you be to drive the massive (and very expensive) vessel blindfolded? Nor would you just look at the space right in front of the ship's bow. You would look *ahead*, toward the horizon.

One of the major responsibilities you actually get paid for in sales is to monitor the horizon. Are the

> **THE ONLY TRUTHFUL PROMISE YOU SHOULD MAKE IF YOU FIND YOURSELF IN A SIMILAR SITUATION SHOULD SOUND LIKE THIS: "NO MATTER WHAT HAPPENS, WE WILL MAKE IT RIGHT."**

waters ahead clear of any obstacles? Have the market winds suddenly shifted, pushing you toward a rocky reef? Has there been a technological shift that might impact your client's business?

You're not only looking at the horizon for your client, but also for yourself. Is the economy heading into a downturn? How is business changing in your market? Where are the winds blowing?

You can't predict everything, which is one of many reasons *why* you should always have an eye on the horizon, gauging your industry. You can see some changes happening, like a storm brewing in the distance. But if you haven't been keeping an eye out, a gust will knock you right on your butt. While you're busy dusting yourself off and figuring out how to react, more *prepared* salespeople will swoop right in and take business away from you.

Instead, you want to be known as a person who is prepared for anything. Your clients should know this about you as well. Tell them you are not only focused on their needs now but you will be prepared for what's coming down the road too. You're not saying you know the future, you're saying you are prepared to handle whatever comes your way. You want them to see you as the voice of calm in the middle of the storm.

To use an example from hunting, you have to pay attention to all the conditions around you: the weather, the time of day, and how much daylight is left. The best time to go bird hunting is in the morning when they're moving about, not the middle of the day. But you only know this if you've been paying attention to the conditions around you. Any change in the natural environment impacts your ability to be successful in the hunt.

Likewise, if you see change approaching on the horizon and you can bring it to the attention of your clients, you will go from being seen as an ordinary salesperson to being a valued *business partner*. Even if your client was already aware of the change and started making their own plans, they will appreciate you being in the game with them—not sitting on the sidelines.

If I'm looking out for your best interests *and* my own versus someone only looking out for their *own* best interest, who would you trust to help steer your ship?

HOW CORPORATE REPUTATION AFFECTS PERSONAL REPUTATION

As you already know, how clients perceive you is vital to your success. What about how they perceive your company, though?

Who you choose to work for is an extension of yourself, even though you are only responsible for your own reputation.

Let's say a client calls you and is upset over a corporate issue, not anything you personally did. Maybe your company ended up in the news for a recall issue or a bad customer interaction was caught on camera and went viral. How do you approach the situation?

First, remember you are representing both sides just like in a negotiation—a lot of those same skills translate here, too. Once you know your client's perspective of the situation, gain clarity from your company, too. Don't simply react to the client's emotions, which will be strong and demanding. It's natural for them to want an answer immediately. Meanwhile, you are only getting a few pieces of the puzzle at a time: what the news is saying, what HR is saying, what your boss is saying, and so on.

In such situations, it's time to use your listening skills. If you don't have an obvious solution in front of you—and most of the time you won't—then pause the discussion with your client and take the issue to your manager or whoever needs to be involved on the corporate side. Buy some time by telling the client, "I agree this is a serious issue. I'm in the process of getting more information and will share more soon." From there, you can bring the puzzle pieces together to form the full picture and reach a positive solution.

Remember, you have to gain understanding and clarity from both sides to even formulate a solid plan. Only after gaining clarity can you have a productive conversation with the client. Your responsibility as a salesperson is to go out there and explain in great detail *exactly* what happened and what steps the company is taking to resolve the issue.

Take an honest approach of "this was a bad thing," never "it's not as bad as it sounds." Recognize the client is unhappy, concerned, and they will need to do what's needed to protect their own business. Whatever they decide won't reflect on you personally.

This is the tough part of the job but a necessary one. You will take the bullets and get yelled at—even when clients know it's not actually your fault. But never belittle their frustration with the events unfolding, and try not to be offended. If they choose to take their business elsewhere, so be it. It doesn't mean they will be gone forever.

CLIENTS WILL COME AND GO, BUT THE ONES WHO STAY AND THE ONES WHO RETURN WILL BE BECAUSE OF *YOUR* REPUTATION.

Communicate you're more interested in *their* business rather than your own business: "I'm here to do whatever I can to help *you* through this difficult situation. If that means you have to take your business elsewhere, I will do whatever I can to ease your transition."

You might be surprised how effective this can be because it's so different from their expectations, especially if they are expecting to hear an excuse. When they come expecting a fight, you offer an olive branch.

Some clients will stay out of loyalty to you. Some will stay for pricing. And some will leave. Regardless, the ones who stay will do so because of what YOU do to keep them. If someone leaves because of a company's mistake, there's a good chance they'll leave your competitor too when THEY make a mistake. You've heard of the "Circle of Life." For some companies, this is just part of the "Circle of Mistakes."

All you can do is go out and *keep hunting*. Clients will come and go, but the ones who stay and the ones who return will be because of *your* reputation.

I lost a big client once due to a complete misunderstanding. Their expectations were for us to pay a sum of money for a mistake we did not even make. There was no changing their perception of the situation.

I didn't give up though.

After discussing the issue with my company, I offered a solution I thought was fair. I asked for time to do some more research and correct the mistake, but the client wasn't interested in alternatives. At this point, my company would not budge any further, either.

So the client left.

Sure, I was disappointed they decided to take their business elsewhere, but for now, there was nothing else I could do. Yet I decided to stay in touch with the disgruntled client from afar, setting up "camp" to watch how things go for them.

Why?

Well, because I know a day will come when my competitor runs into a similar problem with the client. When it happens, I want to be in an advantageous position to reclaim their business.

I view experiences like this one as an educational opportunity. Even though I may have "lost" business, I'm still keeping my eyes on the future. Some salespeople will never think twice about the client they lost. Often, it's a judgment call. Are they worth your time or is your time better spent hunting new opportunities?

I am still learning from mistakes—whether they are mine or someone else's—and gaining valuable experience to this day. No one starts a journey at the finish line. You have to run the race first.

I did not immediately find success when I started out in sales. An even better example is Bill Gates, founder and CEO of Microsoft. He didn't start out as a traditional success story. He was a college dropout, working in a garage, trying to sell software to people who had no idea what the word "software" even meant.

NO ONE STARTS A JOURNEY AT THE FINISH LINE. YOU HAVE TO RUN THE RACE FIRST.

Everyone has to go through the ropes and stages of success. Everyone has their own race to run.

As humans, we can see a successful person and think, "They are so lucky." Are they really though?

Anthony Robbins said it best in his book *Notes from a Friend* where he defines L.U.C.K. as "Labor Under Correct Knowledge."[5] What he's saying is where you start does not matter as much as the decisions you make. Working hard and learning determine where you end up more than chance.

Luck has nothing to do with your determination to succeed. Luck isn't the missing piece to your breakthrough. It can be easy in the world of sales to chalk up success as luck, but how much you *want*

---

5   Robbins, Anthony. *Notes From a Friend* (London: Pocket, 2004), 11.

success is up to you. If you're waiting for a stroke of luck to push you over the top of the bar, well, you might be waiting a long time.

You can't own or control luck, the company, your manager, or your clients. You *can* own and control your reputation.

IT'S NOT COMPLICATED

I understand there are a lot of strategy gurus and experts throughout the sales industry. Each voice is telling you to "do this one thing" or forget another in order to succeed. There's a simple reason for this: we're all different. The sales strategy for one person doesn't work for another. We sell different products to different industries—not to mention to different people. With so many variables, it's impossible to create a perfect recipe for success.

> **YOU CAN'T OWN OR CONTROL LUCK, THE COMPANY, YOUR MANAGER, OR YOUR CLIENTS. YOU *CAN* OWN AND CONTROL YOUR REPUTATION.**

Knowing this, I hope to not just be another voice for you but an honest compass. If you haven't learned this about me already, I am a straightforward kind of guy. I am going to tell you the truth and leave out the fluff.

Sales can be complex, but building your reputation doesn't need to be complicated. In fact, building your reputation is fairly simple when you break everything down.

Think about your own reputation the same way you would judge a company, whether it is good or bad.

For example, let's head back to the car lot for a moment. Some people out there are Ford people or Chevy people. Why?

Reputation. A brand's reputation is the intersection of the buyer's perception and what they value most.

I've yet to meet the person who shows up to the car dealership and says, "I'm buying this car because I listened to an interview with the CEO, and we both like the same flavor of ice cream." People are attached to a particular brand because of how the brand's reputation aligns with what they value, whether it's safety, reliability, low gas mileage, low environmental impact, or communicating a certain level of status. Meanwhile, there are those who care about a company's values—their ethics, employee treatment, wages offered, customer service, and so on.

Branding, perceived value, and reputation are all connected.

In other words, the fundamentals of a good company aren't about the owners' wealth or societal rank. It's about business ethics and how they treat their people. If you treat your clients like they are *your* people, you will have a good reputation.

If you look at building your brand and reputation in these simple terms, the problems you encounter day-to-day should be considered the same way. I've given you many examples so far, but each one can be broken down into a simple format:

Someone's disappointed, somebody didn't do what was expected, and now there needs to be a change.

Seeing each issue in this light eases the pressure and allows you to solve each problem in a unique and efficient way. This statement prompts you to ask, "Who's disappointed? My contact or their boss? What expectation was missed? Was it pricing or performance? What exactly needs to change? And how can I facilitate the change?"

When I graduated from college, I was interviewed for a position in three stages. I passed the first two stages and was asked to take part in the third. During the last stage, three people interviewed me at the same time. Out of the three different interviewers, I was the top choice for two of them—and the second choice for the third.

Turns out there was another candidate they really liked, so the deputy director of the department and his administrative assistant invited both me and the other candidate to lunch for a bonus head-to-head interview.

Obviously this was a bit unconventional, so I wasn't sure what to expect. The interview went on for over two hours. The deputy director would ask me a question, then ask my competition the same question. Once we both answered, he would flip-flop the order and ask another question.

I could feel the pressure rising with each response I gave but I was honest and focused. I tried my best to avoid repeating the same answers as my competitor. The director tried to throw a wrench in my strategy by repeating concepts he already asked us about.

Unlike my competition though, I still offered a unique approach to the repeated questions. I never once said, "As I previously stated..." and never hesitated in re-answering the same questions. My intuition was telling me, "Well, they must not have liked my previous answer, so let's think of a new one."

By bringing a fresh and unique perspective to their questions, I was hired. I truly believe it's because I was able to come up with more than one solution to the same problem. I was able to build a reputation as a creative thinker and problem solver during the interview.

Do you dish out the same answers as the next person? Do you just repeat what you've done before? Or do you dig deeper and take the time to think of each problem as unique? Even if you've seen a problem a hundred times before, how do you approach the issue? If you approach each problem as unique and simplify your solutions as you go, then you will find success in the process.

THE PROCESS VERSUS OUTCOMES

Every problem presents you with a unique opportunity. Remember, there is no such thing as "one solution fits all," no matter how many times you have seen a similar problem crop up. I'm not saying to ignore prior experience. You can use a previous solution as a starting point, but you have to make sure *all* the issues are addressed. Then, you can tweak the issues not addressed and move toward a long-term solution.

By taking an approach like this with a client, you communicate, "I'm listening. I'm working with you and *not* for myself."

On the contrary, if the image you present is "I'm solving the problem just so I can get paid," then you are only looking for easy answers. You're scratching at the surface instead of digging deep. If you take this surface-level approach, do you think you'll be landing any big commissions?

Probably not.

A lot of salespeople overlook this because they get so focused on the *outcome* and not on the *process*. I don't focus on projections; I focus on production. If your process is solid, then the outcome will be too.

IF YOU KEEP FEEDING THE PIPELINE, THE PIPELINE WILL KEEP FEEDING YOU.

When I first started in sales I was told, "Stop focusing on what's coming out at the end of your pipeline. Instead, focus on what's going *into* the pipeline and what's moving forward." If you keep putting stuff into the pipeline, you'll make a good living. If you focus only on what's coming out, you will probably struggle. To put it even simpler, if you keep feeding the pipeline, the pipeline will keep feeding you.

A major reason a lot of salespeople are only focused on the outcomes is bad managers instill this mindset where the only big question they care about is, "What's closing today?" So naturally, everyone is trying to close deals while losing focus on what will bring more deals through the door in the first place.

"Outcomes-only" managers are worried about the health of the company. They are feeling pressure from their own boss, and their boss is feeling pressure from the next rung up on the corporate ladder. Yet, what's not often discussed in the sales industry is how you and the sales manager are on separate missions.

The sales manager's mission is to bring in as much revenue as they can. They do so by squeezing as many dollars out of every deal and cutting as many costs as they can. All so more money goes to the bottom line of the company.

Unfortunately, this is contradictory to what you're trying to do as a salesperson. You're trying to maximize your income and bring business into the company at the same time. The sales manager is only trying to maximize the *company's* income. See the difference?

You can't worry about the health of the company as much as your manager does. Your concern needs to be with the health of the *client*. If your client is healthy, then you are healthy. And if you are healthy, *then* the company is healthy too.

One does not exist without the other, though. There is no sales manager without a sales force and no sales force without a sales manager.

So if you find yourself dealing with an outcomes-driven manager, all you can do is focus on your own goals. If the company needs to make twenty million a month, don't put twenty million pounds of pressure on your shoulders.

Instead, what is *your* goal?

Whatever it is, reach *your* goal. You can't be responsible for everyone else on your team. You are responsible for yourself and your clients.

You're going to have bad sales managers, and you're going to have great ones. You can't control how your manager manages, right? But as I've said before, you *can* control your reputation through any tough circumstance.

I once had a horrible manager who came out with me on a couple of customer visits. I never expected how one day could negatively impact my business. The first client we visited didn't like my manager's attitude. The next customer told me, "Mike, never bring your manager into my office again." The third client canceled their account on the spot.

Talk about a bad day.

My takeaway was to keep treating my job like my own business, and I would find a way to rebuild. Somehow, I would work around the damage my manager did in one day of visits.

Honestly, I still hold a grudge over losing the client, but there was nothing I could do. I couldn't control how my manager interacted with them. The only thing I could control was how I responded. I could only control my reputation, not my manager's.

INTEGRITY IS BASED ON YOUR ABILITY TO BELIEVE IN YOURSELF.

The most important part? Strive for consistency no matter where you are. I work hard to make sure my personal reputation is also my professional reputation.

Your reputation has to be what you believe about yourself. It's never a mask to put on and take off whenever you feel like it. Before you can expect to convince anyone else about what you can deliver, you have to convince yourself. You have to sell the value of your product *to yourself* first. Integrity is based on your ability to believe in yourself. If you don't believe what you're selling will actually benefit anyone, then why are you attaching your reputation to it?

You must wholeheartedly believe you can help others solve their problems, that you offer the best solution for them. Only then can you truly stand out from the crowd as a trusted partner with a sterling reputation. This will keep you from blindly following the crowd as an ineffective Sales Clone rather than a successful Sales Hunter. When I did this for myself, I was able to build a reputation where the hard times didn't keep me down—they were the times that lifted me up the most.

CHAPTER 8

DON'T FOLLOW THE CROWD

During a fire emergency, would you give up just because the exits are blocked or someone told you there was no hope of escape? Of course not! You would find another way out no matter what.

I know escaping a fire might be an extreme example, but it's the truth. As humans, we have a remarkable ability to overcome even the most challenging situations. We shouldn't allow an obstacle to keep us from living and finding success. It's what we do as humans—we survive.

I shared a story earlier in the book I want to dive a bit deeper into. In 2007, during the market crisis, I was confronted with a pivotal moment in my career. The company I worked for—and my entire sales career—was dependent on the housing market. I was responsible for procuring business from builders who were both constructing and selling homes. However, when the market crashed, most new construction and sales came to a screeching halt—and my business was left vulnerable, trapped in the figurative burning building.

Before the crisis even began, the writing was on the wall. But for whatever reason, everyone chose to ignore the warnings. No one wanted to acknowledge the fire alarm was flashing.

The first early signs of trouble were how easily loans were being issued. From my perspective, there were so many unqualified people receiving their third or fourth property investment loans as if they were going to an ATM for grocery money. I made notes to myself, "Write down these addresses—they're going to go bad."

You see, the red flags are always there—they stand out. However, no one pays attention to them when times are good. They only acknowledge them after the crash. So when the crash came, I didn't sit idly by and allow the change to overwhelm and cloud my judgment. Instead, I followed what the landscape was telling me. I survived by asking myself a simple question: "Where can I build a new niche?"

At this point, I had a critical choice to make. I could either give up and surrender to the changing conditions or find a way to adapt to the market. I chose to adapt. As I mentioned before, I started my own notary business, but this wasn't the only path I created for myself. I realized the more avenues of income I made, the better chance of survival during extreme market conditions. Always have more than one fire exit since you never know which way the flames might spread.

ALWAYS HAVE MORE THAN ONE FIRE EXIT SINCE YOU NEVER KNOW WHICH WAY THE FLAMES MIGHT SPREAD.

Rather than focusing on the shrinking pool of builders like everyone else did, I expanded my business into other pools of opportunity. To most, leaving the last strand of security or moving away from what you know during a crisis sounds insane. Even when animals are feeling pressured or afraid, they will refuse to leave their food source to try to find another.

But I wasn't like most people, and to be a successful Sales Hunter, you can't be either. I knew I needed to think and act differently from the crowd to survive. So I learned the ins and outs of receivership and how to navigate bankruptcy courts. Even though I had no prior experience with either, I dove headfirst into the deep end and did a crash course as quickly as possible. Once I felt as comfortable as I could in such a short amount of time, I hit the ground running.

By adapting, I learned how to sell bankrupted properties being resold to the court-appointed receivers. I made myself and my company a lot of money while the rest of the industry was fighting over a very small pool of available products.

I created an exit strategy when the emergency exit was blocked. I removed the last strand of security I had, even though everything inside of me—and everyone around me—wanted to do the opposite. Because I didn't follow the crowd, I not only survived but thrived.

To this day, my reputation in the company is "hard times are usually Mike's best times." I'll take this reputation any day of the week.

When the sun is shining and the birds are singing, it's easy to become complacent and assume everything will always be smooth sailing. However, just like the weather, business conditions can change in the blink of an eye, leaving the unprepared scrambling to find a way out of the storm.

BECAUSE I DIDN'T FOLLOW THE CROWD, I NOT ONLY SURVIVED BUT THRIVED.

You have to be proactive. Start looking for potential problems even when everything *seems* to be going well. Where are the pitfalls lurking? Where are the cracks in the foundation? By identifying these red flags ahead of time, you can take steps to avoid them before they become a real problem.

The crowd might tell you not to be so paranoid. But better to be a little paranoid than lulled into a false sense of security. Because when (not if) the market dips again, you'll be the one who's prepared for the chaos. Chaos usually means a crash and burn situation is near. Running in the middle of chaos is like running during a sugar high. As soon as the sugar wears off, you're done for. You crash and you're out of the race.

Therefore, be the person who takes the extra steps when times are good. Be the one who's always looking for ways to improve, to stay ahead of the curve, and to anticipate the unexpected. Because in business, as in life, the crowd waits for the storm to pass. While they wait, you could use the storm as an opportunity to thrive in the rain.

THE DIGITAL LANDSCAPE

In today's world, we are surrounded not only by people we interact with daily but also by the multitude of voices vying for our attention online. The digital era has unquestionably transformed the way we live, work, and communicate. Access to technology has opened doors to endless opportunities and has brought forth an era of digital entrepreneurship. However, with this new and ever-changing landscape comes a flood of both good *and* bad advice from "experts" who have found success in their industries.

"Sales Gurus," as I like to call them, can be found with a simple search on Google or YouTube. As exciting as the digital age has been, particularly in sales, it's vital to use caution. With one click of your mouse, you suddenly have access to the endless opinions of other sales professionals who claim to have the secret formula for success, many of whom promise you an easy path to riches.

But here's the catch: *their* success story may not be *your* success story. Also, their path may not have been so easy as it initially sounds. Their formula may have worked for them, but that doesn't mean it will work for you. Avoid the urge to "copy and paste" someone else's success, hoping their results will also be yours. Approach everything you read or hear with critical thinking by asking yourself:

"Can their ideas work with my life and experiences?"

"Can I be profitable with this system?"

"What can I control and what can I *not* control?"

These are essential questions to consider when sifting through all the information available at your fingertips. Do your due diligence before you act.

If you're having trouble deciphering which strategies are worth your time and which ones are not, the answer is simple: you are the captain of your own ship and responsible for your own destiny. That thought alone is a significant reason why I wrote this book. This book isn't about getting rich quickly because, let's face it, those books *never* work. It's about creating the lifestyle and mindset that keeps you at the forefront of your industry.

What I want to share with you is a way to simplify sales, a way to think, and a process to get you headed in the *right* direction, not the *same* direction as everyone

> **THIS BOOK ISN'T ABOUT GETTING RICH QUICKLY BECAUSE, LET'S FACE IT, THOSE BOOKS *NEVER* WORK. IT'S ABOUT CREATING THE LIFESTYLE AND MINDSET THAT KEEPS YOU AT THE FOREFRONT OF YOUR INDUSTRY.**

else. Unlike "Sales Gurus," I don't want to provide you with all the answers, and I especially don't want to promise you riches. I'm not you or in your industry, so it would be dishonest of me to claim to have all the answers for you.

But is wealth possible? Absolutely!

Success in sales isn't some whimsical far-off dream. You can achieve it if you want it. I want you to build your own business from the tools you already have available at your disposal. My experiences are not your experiences. My knowledge is not your knowledge. I can't tell you exactly how to sell your product or service, but I can tell you how to approach the common situations you'll encounter in this industry so you can get the most out of your career.

The point I'm trying to make is for you to ask yourself questions like: "What is *my* way?" Or "How do I cater these practices to *my* ability?" If I tell you to deliver every sales pitch in French, and you don't speak French, you're out of luck. Instead, follow the thoughts I give you and develop them for yourself. Mold them to who you are and your natural abilities.

A great way to do this is by thinking about how you were raised, whether it was by a single parent, both parents, or no parents. Your upbringing contributed to who you are, for both the good and the bad. Those experiences helped make you an individual with unique thoughts and valuable ideas. Use your uniqueness to your benefit.

Remember, who you are and what you want to be is the value of your brand and reputation. Be true to yourself. If you are authentic, then you are trustworthy. If you display both of those attributes, people will naturally flock to you. Inauthenticity is the worst mask you could wear. If it were a Halloween costume, it would be the Groucho Marx glasses and bushy mustache. Everyone can see right through the cheap disguise.

If you want to be someone else, then you aren't confident in your own abilities. If you aren't confident, why would any client have the confidence to entrust you with their business? Inauthenticity only creates distance and tension between you and your clients. There's no "one-size-fits-all" person for a "one-size-fits-all" solution. This is precisely why *you*, the individual, is needed. You need to figure out what works best for you.

Growing up, I had a desire to work in medical or biological sciences. But I soon discovered the main core studies consisted of complicated mathematics.

To put it bluntly, I am terrible at math and failed miserably. Mostly because I've always been a bit of a rebel and loved to create a different spin on things, make ideas my own, and create solutions no one had thought of before. So I shifted gears and majored in political science and minored in history instead.

Frankly, I'm not good at following a predetermined set of rules, and math is nothing but rules. I was more interested in learning how to take the facts presented, amass them, and create an argument. I tend to operate more from the belief that every rule of life can be supported or worked around where there is disagreement. In other words, rather than prove to you that "2+2=4," I'd rather discuss why "4" even matters to you. What do you get out of "4" which "3" doesn't give to you? Should we be looking at "5" as an option for you instead? Rather than be stuck on the rules, let's talk about what you value. This is why I personally don't love strict sales scripts.

For me, finding the individuality, the exceptions to the rules, is the beauty of the process. If I had tried to be someone I wasn't, I don't think I would've experienced the success I have. Everyone is going to try to tell you how to do your job—your manager, peers, family, and friends. They all mean well, but the best way to do anything is the way that works in your style, your voice.

We're all human, we're all different, and we all look at things through a unique perspective. There's no one way to be. No one way to find success in your field like the online Sales Gurus like to teach. Can you still learn from them? Sure. You might find something that fits your style perfectly. You might also learn what *not* to do. Take the time to visualize whether you can see yourself actually doing what is being taught.

So as you embark on your own journey, remember to be a little bit of a rebel and find your own way. Take advice from those you trust, take the advice from this book, but don't be afraid to question the many voices vying for your attention. At the end of the day, when the noise of the day goes silent, you'll only have yourself.

RULES VERSUS SUGGESTIONS

For sales professionals who love using formulas and following rules, don't worry—there are plenty of opportunities for finding success as a Sales Hunter for you, too. Whether you use this book as a guide or follow it strictly as a rule book is entirely up to you. Regardless of how you view this content, the key takeaway is you'll learn to think more critically about your sales process and develop your own unique approach that benefits both you and your clients.

Every individual perceives the world and information through their own unique lens. For example, consider driving. Not everyone follows the speed limit perfectly, right? Some people adhere to it strictly or even choose to stay below. Others know there is usually a bit of leeway to go over, depending on the area and the risk they are willing to accept.

For example, I personally view parking signs as suggestions only. My kids always laugh at me when I pull into a "20-minute parking spot" in front of a busy restaurant. Sure, I might get a ticket or get yelled at by the restaurant owner, but I'm willing to take the risk for the reward. I'd much rather spend my time *in* the restaurant than looping around a parking lot for thirty minutes waiting for a spot to open up. The way I see it is the restaurant offered me a suggestion, and I chose not to accept it.

I am not here to judge anyone for following the sign as a rule. Every individual bases decisions on one of two things: willingness to accept potential pain, or avoidance of potential pain. No matter what the scenario, you have to deal with the results of your choices.

I'm willing to take on the potential pain of viewing most rules as suggestions and exploring different veins of opportunity a rule follower may not see. For someone else who is inclined to follow the rules, they simply do not want to risk the potential pain involved because of the stress it gives them. And that's totally fine! Some thrive on the freedom of exploring uncharted territory, while others prefer the reassuring structure of following tried-and-true guidelines.

SOME THRIVE ON THE FREEDOM OF EXPLORING UNCHARTED TERRITORY, WHILE OTHERS PREFER THE REASSURING STRUCTURE OF FOLLOWING TRIED-AND-TRUE GUIDELINES.

There are pros and cons to both methods. For those of us who choose a more unconventional path, we may find ourselves in some strange situations or even make a simple situation more complicated than it needs to be. On the other hand, the rule follower can often find solutions more quickly by relying on established guidelines.

In the end, both methods have a place and can lead to success. Regardless of which approach you choose, there will always be moments of pain in sales. Losing a client can be a tough pill to swallow. Yet you must remember they are always making a choice for what they perceive as best for them. The choice to leave your company might cause them less pain in the future than if they stayed. The important part is to recognize your own "pain tolerance" as a key factor in determining outcomes throughout your career. If you can act with this awareness of yourself, it will allow you to forge your own path.

LEADING WITH A TARGET ON YOUR BACK

When you forge your own path within a system designed to keep everyone going in the same direction, there will naturally be a target on your back. People will want to know why you're choosing to be different. Do you know something they don't? Is your way the better way? When you don't follow the crowd, you're going to stick out.

However, having a target on your back may indicate your business is moving forward, rather than simply going with the flow. By seeing the world and market in a new way, you bring fresh ideas and perspective to a stagnant system. You provide others with a different yet effective result.

I'm not saying you should try to be different just for the sake of standing out. That's not the solution. *Authenticity* is key in sales, period. Inauthenticity will be toxic to your business. Instead, by embracing your uniqueness and providing unique solutions, you can set yourself apart and be a leader in your industry.

But how do you stay on top?

Let's look at IBM. When they first began their business, they revolutionized the computer industry by making computing more accessible. At the time, computers were only used by large tech corporations and businesses. Not many imagined one could be brought into their home or office. However, IBM saw an opportunity and provided a product for the masses, disrupting the industry.

As a result, a big ol' target was painted on their back, yet they remained at the forefront for a while. However, companies like Apple and Microsoft soon came along, assessed what IBM was doing—and more importantly, what IBM *wasn't* doing. Instead of copying IBM's formula, they thought "We could do better. We can be different." And they were right.

Today, IBM is no longer thought of as a computer company, while Microsoft and Apple dominate the market. But it's possibly a matter of time until someone else comes along, looks at what they are doing, and finds a different, better way.

So how long you stay at the forefront, like everything else in sales, is often a choice. How long are you willing to pay the price, endure the pain, or walk with a target on your back? Once you're at the front, you can never take your foot off the gas. You can't follow what the crowd is trending toward because you're at the front of the crowd. *You* have to make the trend.

Why do you think Apple is constantly making new products? Why is Microsoft always improving their software and developing AI technology?

They want to set the bar where *they* can control it. They are the trendsetters while IBM has transformed into new spaces for their own survival.

There will always be nuances and variables out of your control. However, by focusing on what you *can* control, you can set yourself apart and become a leader in your industry.

What is everyone else in your industry complaining about? Start there. Instead of complaining, be the one coming up with solutions. The crowd complains. The victors forge new paths.

If you want to be at the forefront, you have to look at your market, all flowing in the same direction, and see where the gaps are.

THE CROWD COMPLAINS. THE VICTORS FORGE NEW PATHS.

Where are the areas that need change or where an update is needed? Once you discover those areas, the next question to ask yourself is, "How can I make this better?" After that, "How can I provide this in a way no one else has?" The answers are already within you—you just have to find the opportunity to bring them out. The crowd will never do it for you.

CHAPTER 9

NUANCES WITHIN SALES

As I mentioned at the end of the last chapter, part of why I can't—and shouldn't—give anyone an exact recipe is because I'm not you and you're not me. We aren't selling the same product or service. We're not paid the same. We're not dealing with exactly the same clientele. Even in my own sales history, I've had to adjust my own style for new situations. Mike the Sales Hunter of today isn't exactly the same as Mike the Sales Hunter from five years ago.

As a hunter visualizes their prey and their hunt before venturing into the wilderness, they still cannot predict exactly what will happen. Even the most experienced hunters can still get rattled. That's what makes the wilderness *wild*. The unpredictability, the unknown, and the struggle to survive. Yet, those same things are what make hunters keep coming back for more, because each time they venture out into the unknown, they get stronger, wiser, and more experienced. Similarly, in life and business, we must sometimes take a leap of faith and venture into the unknown to improve.

During my mid-twenties, I found myself in the corporate wilderness. I left my public service job with the County of Riverside to work for a commercial company on a commission-only basis. At the time, I was going through a divorce and I was in a mental funk. I was a single homeowner without the safety net of a second income, so I had to find a way to pay my bills and stay afloat.

For several months, like Tom Hanks in the movie *Castaway*, all my energy was focused on survival. I even got a roommate to help with expenses. And no, he wasn't a volleyball with a face painted on him. Even so, I still needed to create a path for self-sufficiency, so when another opportunity for a commission-only sales position presented itself, I took the chance. At first, I was hesitant because my previous experience with a commission-only structure had been a failure. But this time, I decided to push all my chips in and give the role all my attention and effort. I had nothing else to lose. I needed to forge a path and this job gave me the kick in the butt I needed to push myself.

I know I shared this story before but it's time for some additional context here. After the first sixty days in my new position, I hadn't taken a single day off, not even weekends or holidays. My performance was strong, but my coworkers felt different about my hustle, which led to an important lesson from my sales manager.

He sat me down and said, "Mike, your priorities are not their priorities." Initially, I was confused by what he meant, but through that conversation, I learned two valuable philosophies:

A. Feed the pipeline, and the pipeline will feed you.

B. *Your* motivations as a salesperson are not necessarily the same as those of your coworkers.

At first, I didn't fully comprehend the implications of these lessons, but as time went on, they became clearer. The sense of urgency

I carried with me at all times was interpreted by my coworkers as being rude and impatient. Why would they work on the weekend just because I was? Why should they drop everything they are doing to process *my* order? Especially if I was coming across as disrespectful?

This way of doing things was not only unproductive but also counterintuitive. I couldn't control the pace at which orders were processed, and my colleagues were not obligated to cater to my demands. They had their own priorities to consider.

I was so outcome-focused that I neglected what was going *in* the pipeline. My priorities shifted, and I learned to let go of the things that were beyond my control.

I learned my expectations needed to stay with me and not get put on anyone else. I needed to focus on filling my figurative wheelbarrow with as much treasure as possible. So I channeled my energy toward seeking new opportunities and put in the necessary effort to make them happen.

Even with these realizations setting me on the right track, it was still a tough time. I found myself paying my Visa with a Mastercard and transferring money between accounts just to get by. However, I couldn't let this temporary trek through the wilderness get in the way of my long-term goals.

Despite the challenges, I don't regret my decision to work on a commission-only basis. It forced me to work smarter, harder, and become proficient at my job quickly. I learned the value of what I was making, how to budget, and how to handle unexpected setbacks. Though I had no safety net, I emerged from the wilderness experience a better salesperson—and a more resilient person in general.

When I started my career in sales, I quickly discovered this industry had many nuances which deserve careful consideration. Among the most critical of these nuances was understanding the different types of compensation structures. Two popular types of compensation in sales are commission-only and salary with commission. Both have their pros and cons, and like everything else in sales, there is no one-size-fits-all solution. In this chapter, we will explore both and other essential distinctions to help you gain the perspective needed to succeed.

COMMISSION-ONLY PAY STRUCTURE

Think back to history class and you might recall a few facts about Alexander the Great. You might remember he conquered much of the Mediterranean world before his death, but did you know he can also teach us a thing or two about commission-only sales? Well, maybe in not a conventional way, but if you learned anything about me yet, I'm not too conventional either.

To give you a quick historical recap, Alexander was only twenty when he inherited his throne and set out to expand his empire at any cost. When his armies reached the Middle East, they were ready to head home. They had marched across the known globe, conquered countless lands, and gained overwhelming wealth in the process. They wanted to climb aboard some boats and head straight back for Greece.

But Alexander had other plans in mind. He wanted them to *march* back the way they came, continue their conquest, and leave no stone unturned.

As you can imagine, the exhausted army was not happy with Alexander's idea of "going home." They probably thought, "Why can't we just sail back and enjoy our newfound treasures?"

Alexander had other plans. He knew if he allowed his army to get comfortable and complacent for the remainder of the war campaign, their efforts would be for nothing in the long run.

One night, while the army was camped, he went out and burned every single boat down to the frame, leaving a pile of smoldering ash in the waters. This left his army no choice but to follow him wherever he led them next.

Now, let's apply this idea to commission-only sales. When you commit to a commission-only lifestyle, you are essentially burning the boats. There is no salary safety net, no guaranteed income. You have to be all-in, committed to the job, and willing to do whatever it takes to succeed. This type of position quickly weeds out the weak, and if you stick around long enough, learn what you can, and put your knowledge into action, it makes you a better salesperson.

Yes, it will be tough. But ultimately, it's also very rewarding. Just like Alexander the Great, some days you have to take a bold approach and burn the boats. This forces you to focus on the present and gives you the drive to succeed. In the end, the challenges and hardships you face will make you a stronger, more resilient salesperson, and the rewards will be well worth it.

Remember, bigger risk equals bigger reward. Isn't that the case with most big decisions we face in our lives? If you take the leap of faith and commit to a commission-only structure, you will see the benefits in the long run. The skills you will learn are valuable and the money you make will be greater too.

But is commission-only the right choice for you? This is what only you can answer for yourself.

SALARY WITH COMMISSION PAY STRUCTURE

Many people in sales positions have the option of being paid a salary *with* commissions. This means in addition to a base salary, they also earn commissions based on their sales performance. Although the commissions are smaller than those in a commission-only position, a successful Sales Hunter will still see commissions make up most of their income in this payment structure. For most in this industry, the base salary only makes 25–33 percent of the entire paycheck.

For starters, having a salary provides some regular income, which can be helpful for those who need the consistency to support themselves and their families. If you are just starting out in sales, a salary plus commission structure might benefit you as you learn the basics of the job.

With a base salary, you might not have to work sixty-hour weeks and you can afford to take a day or two off. Trust me, there were days I wished I had a salary to fall back on instead of feeling defeated after a long day with no commission to show for it. The mental grind of continuing to show up with no guaranteed reward can be stressful to say the least. Even if the salary is a small amount, having a guaranteed paycheck can provide some peace of mind. Sometimes it's a good mental boost to feel rewarded for your effort.

So if you are just starting out and want to hone your skills, learn the lay of the industry, and need to offset the mental stress of finding a sale right away, a salary plus commission structure might benefit you the most.

However, you must be aware of the downsides to being paid a salary plus commissions, especially for someone who has already mastered their industry or business. In this case, if you're more seasoned and have a decent pipeline working for you, you may be better off switching to a commission-only structure where you can earn a higher percentage.

While having a base salary may remove some financial anxiety, it may also make someone *too* comfortable. Think about the story of burning the boats. With a base salary, you may be able to cruise along comfortably for longer than someone who's on commission-only. But is comfort really the best way to grow and succeed in sales? Maybe for a time, but in the long run, you are going to have to make the trek through the wilderness. This book is about setting up your sales career as your *own* business—and there's no base salary for the entrepreneur!

What's important is for you to analyze your own needs and personality to determine whether a base salary makes sense for you. Are you the type who needs a salary for stability, or are you comfortable taking risks to gain the rewards of commission-only?

For example, a married individual without a second income may need the base salary because they need to make sure their family is taken care of. On the other hand, a married individual whose spouse brings in a second income may be comfortable with commission-only because at least they have one predictable income. Or they may think of it the other way and be able to rely on a salary plus commission structure more than someone who is single and needs to support themselves entirely through their sales. Again, these are personal preferences where you have to decide what makes the most sense for your situation and personality.

Overall, if you have the wherewithal and drive, the rewards of a commission plus salary structure can be high. However, it's important to remember no matter what your pay structure is, your philosophies and strategies should remain the same. It's up to you to continue to learn, grow, and adapt in order to succeed in sales.

COMPANY STRUCTURE

A company structure is an important aspect to understand before you get to work. Just like the pay structure, each business is laid out in a specific way. In terms of general company structure, organizations can either be siloed or non-siloed. A siloed organization is structured in a way where they have different departments functioning separately, often with some level of communication or collaboration between them. On the other hand, a non-siloed organization doesn't have different departments at all.

The majority of companies are siloed, aside from extremely small businesses. To clarify, the bigger the company, the more silos it will have. The smaller the company, the less likely it is to be siloed. Are there exceptions? Of course. But by and large, this holds true.

Being part of a large, siloed organization can often provide numerous opportunities for growth and development. As someone who has worked a long time in such an environment, I can attest to some of the wonderful benefits. But because of the size, we also encounter many challenges, especially in terms of communication and consistency.

The main challenge I see is clients who may not understand the nuances of the business structure and expect consistency across *all* silos. The way they see it is "I'm doing business with XYZ Company," and so they expect the entire company to be on the same page across the board. Funny thing is, they often think this way even if they are also working for a siloed organization themselves!

Consistency across silos isn't necessarily impossible to achieve. In fact, establishing the understanding of your company being on the same page with your client is the right thing to do. But with one minor miscommunication, this expectation can easily create difficulties for your client and yourself, especially in large organizations where clients may interact with different silos and receive varying levels of service.

When working in a siloed organization, it's important to figure out how to meet the customer's needs while still selling the value of the company. This means you have to strike a balance between meeting the customer's needs while not blaming other silos for any issues that arise.

At the same time, when you involve management in any situation where a client ends up in another silo, your manager will be looking at *you* for an answer as to why the client ended up there. They might ask something like, "Why didn't you have enough control over your client to keep them in your silo? Haven't you told them to reach out to you directly?"

These situations happen all the time and can happen to anyone. It's almost always a misunderstanding of the company structure. For instance, imagine you sold a client a bunch of purple widgets, and the shipment is running late. Naturally, the client wants to know where their product is, but maybe this particular client decides not to bother you. They know you're not in charge of packaging and shipping, so they decide to pull up the company website, see a number for the Shipping and Receiving department, and give them a call.

To your client, they may think they are saving both of you time in a situation like this. But what they don't understand is how something so simple can quickly become complicated.

Before you know it, your client is interacting with a completely different silo who is unaware of the connection already established. Let's say the warehouse manager is the one who answers the call. He doesn't interact with customers on a daily basis and his only concern is getting goods out the door.

So when your client asks about their order, they aren't thinking about the thousands of other orders pending and all the other stuff happening in the warehouse. But the warehouse manager *is* thinking about the thousands of other orders, and maybe he is a little short with your client. Most likely, because the warehouse manager is wondering why the client called the warehouse—why didn't they just call you, the sales rep? Once this eventually comes back to you—because it will—you are now responsible for fixing it.

This once minor issue has now grown into a bigger one. Your customer is not just wondering about the shipment being late, but now they're also upset over how they were treated by the warehouse—especially since they still don't know where their order is! See how situations in a siloed organization can become easily tangled?

Either way, you still need to understand what happened so your manager is in the loop too. Because trust me, your manager will want to know why the warehouse was on the phone with an established client.

So if your contact *does* end up interacting with a different silo, when you inquire about how they ended up there, your tone can't be accusatory. This sounds obvious, I know, but you'd be surprised how easy it is to do, especially if you're naturally sarcastic like I am.

I had a client call me up one day and ask about an issue. I wasn't finding the request on my end but found it tangled up with another silo who was also working on resolving the same issue.

"Why did you go to them for help?" I asked a bit too bluntly.

I meant it as a joke, but the customer became angry with me, thinking I was blaming them for the issue. Looking back now, I can understand why!

NEVER MAKE YOUR PROBLEM THE CUSTOMER'S PROBLEM.

It's crucial to handle these situations with caution and care. Never make your problem the customer's problem. As we have discussed throughout this book, reputation is *everything* in sales, so it's essential to keep proving who you are to maintain a positive reputation and brand.

Remember when silo issues arise, it's going to rattle the client's expectations. Even if another silo has messed up, it's also the wrong approach to throw them under the bus. Doing so not only means putting yourself into conflict with another silo you depend on, but it also means the customer's perspective may shift to seeing the company as inept.

Once a client ends up in another silo, it's likely to happen again. The best thing you can do is to go learn the key players in the different silos and find out what they do so you can prevent future issues. Learning to work with other silos, gaining their support, and having them as advocates will only help you down the road! Internal networking like this can be just as valuable as external networking.

Sharing with other silos how valuable their assistance is in the grand scheme of the business can make you more knowledgeable about how the company works. The more you know, the more you can help your client when a silo issue arises. This only increases your value to them as a problem solver!

CHANGING POINT OF SALES

Establishing a long-term relationship with your clients is undoubtedly crucial. However, there's another vital aspect of sales which cannot be overlooked: the point of sale. For many account executives, you not only lead the customer through the sales process, but continue to service the customer for the life of the account.

But for others, there may be less points of contact. Maybe after closing the deal, the account is moved to a customer success team. Still for others, like in a retail store, there is literally only a single point-of-sales contact with the customer—the few minutes they are at the sales counter to check out!

Many entry-level sales positions are centered around these critical single interactions, whether in a retail store, door-to-door sales, or even online advertising. Here's the thing—many of the concepts covered in this book apply even if you're only dealing with a single point of contact. In fact, I aim to change the way you approach single point-of-contact sales and rethink these one-off interactions entirely!

Your first job as a sales professional is to help the customer understand what they're looking for and what value they're seeking. From there, you can help them identify the benefits and value of your products. While these basics of sales are well-known and typically well-covered in any sales training, remember they remain the same throughout your career, regardless of position or fancy title.

The bottom line in any sales position is that a deal isn't done until it's done.

It's like baseball. You aren't out until you are *called* out. It's important you run through the base, until you're actually tagged out. You never know what could happen. You'll see the pros do it all the time. They will hit an easy ground ball but still hustle over to first and run all the way through the base even if they were already thrown out.

Why?

Well, the infielder could overthrow the ball and an easy out becomes a base hit because you were prepared. Either way, you *always* run it out in sales too.

Since many single point-of-sales interactions involve one-off customers, you usually don't have to worry about following up. Or, to continue with the baseball analogy, you're not worried about getting on second or third base.

During a single point-of-sale interaction, the customer typically selects the product, color, or other details, and you ring them up before handing them their purchase. Sale is done and over. In fact, unless there is an issue with the product and the customer returns to the store, you're not required to follow up or do anything else. You ran it out and closed the deal. "Next!"

But what if you took a different approach? What if you approached every customer interaction as if they were a repeat customer, even if they're not? What if you put on your Sales Hunter cap for a second and changed the way you approached every single point-of-contact interaction? Ask yourself, "Is there even such a thing as a single point of sale?"

It all goes back to how you interact with your customers whether it be at a clothing retailer or on a car lot. If someone walks into a store to buy some pants and you help them, answer their questions, and provide a solution to their problem, then what's the likelihood they will come back and be a repeat customer?

I'd say very likely.

Conversely, if you treat customers as a one-off sale, you'll likely create a one-off customer. By approaching every interaction as an opportunity to create a repeat customer, you open the door to more opportunities and more money in your pocket.

Because the key difference between single point-of-sale contact and a long-term contact is what happens *after* we get on first base. For most single point-of-sale professionals, that's it, it's over. Meanwhile, the long-term sales reps are just getting started. They are thinking of setting up the next meeting, checking in with the client on their goals for the next quarter, and so on. They are looking for how they can serve the customer so well, the account continues to provide more value.

What do you have to lose in single point-of-contact sales by thinking long term? Literally nothing. But you have a lot to gain. Especially when the one-off customer becomes a loyal customer and tells your manager how great you are. Or what if the customer is a sales director at a company and recognizes your skill? You'd be surprised by the job offers that have happened from such single interactions!

REFERRALS

If you think of your sales career as your own business then your ultimate objective is to expand. Referrals are one of the best ways you can achieve this in a swift and efficient manner. However, referrals are not something you can simply expect from your clients—they must be *earned*.

Imagine yourself in your client's shoes for a moment. If you received a service that exceeded your expectations, would you not eagerly recommend it to your friends? But what if the service was just average, without any real added spark? The likelihood of you recommending it to others would be considerably lower. No one recommends the restaurant they thought was "alright." They recommend the one that blew their socks off!

In order to receive referrals yourself, you have to leave a spark— make a lasting impression. Simply doing your job is not enough. You need to go above and beyond to prove your value and establish your reputation as what you say it is. In other words, *prove it*. Asking for referrals without having a base for it eliminates all the good work you already did. Just like any business owner, you have to earn everything.

A good practice that should be in everyone's repertoire is knowing WHEN to ask for a referral compared to HOW you ask. For instance, after you just completed excellent service for the customer or solved a really complex issue, you've proved your value and proved your brand and reputation. This is a perfect window of opportunity to seek a referral.

Never overestimate the power of word-of-mouth either. Remember, your reputation will be in rooms even when you aren't physically there. Clients will talk with other potential clients.

I once attended a networking event with a satisfied customer who introduced me to a key decision-maker at another organization. My client asked, "Who are you doing business with?" Turned out they were working with one of my colleagues. Despite this, my customer urged the DM to work with me instead.

That's about as good as it gets in sales! Now, don't worry—I didn't poach a client from my colleague. Ethics before commission. But what if instead of a colleague, it had been my competition? You better believe I would've developed a game plan to gain his business and given him a call!

When you establish strong relationships and deliver exceptional service, whether in a single point of contact or a long-term account you're servicing, success and growth will follow. Whether you are in a siloed organization or non-siloed, whether you are commission-only or salary plus commission, the same holds true. At the end of the day, it all comes down to how you choose to establish yourself and build *your* business. With determination and persistence, the opportunities to expand your business are endless.

CHAPTER 10

AS YOUR BUSINESS GROWS

One of my business idols is Lee Iacocca, the late automotive executive known for helping develop the Ford Mustang and reviving the Chrysler Corporation when he became its CEO during the 1980s. If you've seen the 2019 movie *Ford v Ferrari*, he was portrayed by actor Jon Bernthal. From my perspective, his success was rooted in knowing the value of his time and exactly what he could bring to the table.

In his autobiography, *Iacocca*, he told the story of being a young executive at Ford, going into a meeting early, and waiting for a prospect to arrive. Fifteen minutes after the meeting was supposed to start, with no sign of the prospect, another executive suggested, "Let's get out of here."

Iacocca was flabbergasted. "Why? This is a really important meeting!"

The executive responded, "This is a very important meeting to *us* but obviously not to our prospect. We need to rethink our approach."

He learned a valuable lesson from the executive that day. He learned what they had to offer in the meeting wasn't being valued by the client. Otherwise, the client would've been on time. The other executive's suggestion to rethink their approach was all about value—figuring out what they could offer that would compel the prospect to be on time, ready to talk. While you can't control how everyone perceives the value you offer, you *can* take control of who you offer value to.

If a client isn't going to take you seriously, should you place any value on them? If so, how much is too much? Is there some sort of value gauge to use?

Well, of course there is.

Think of it a bit like a pressure gauge when airing up your tires. If a tire is already full, does it need more? No. You'll only do damage trying to add more. Instead, your time and attention is better spent on the tires which need to be filled. In the same way, you need to gauge where you can actually add value.

WHERE DO YOU ADD VALUE?

Not everyone will value what you're offering. But if your goal is to bring value to everything you do, to take pride in your work, then don't waste time with the people who don't value you, your time, or your service. It's important to be selective with your clients and to work with people who appreciate your expertise and your brand. Focus on the tasks important to growing your business and achieving your long-term goals.

In order to keep myself aligned with my own goals, I see my life coach every other Friday. During our meetings, I inevitably receive multiple phone calls. On the surface, I know this sounds rude, but it's actually part of our agreement. Her job as a life coach is to value what I value, to help me maintain and improve upon my reputation.

She knows if one of my clients has an emergency, it's my personal value to "take the call." So to make the most of our time, I carry two phones—one which I ignore during our session if it rings, and the other one which I answer if it goes off. Because customer care is one of my values, she's complemented this ability to stay focused on whoever is in front of me without neglecting my values.

To some, having two phones might seem like an extra distraction, especially in the digital age. And for some people, it might be. But I know myself well enough, I am actually more organized with two phones. Because I am more organized, I'm also more prepared for problems when they arise.

If I know a client is going to be calling me, I want them to know they will have my undivided attention no matter what. If I see a number pop up and I already know it's not urgent, I won't answer.

You see, I understand the value of my time, and if I waste it, then I'm setting myself and my clients up for failure. Wasted time does not bring value to my life or my business.

BE THE CLEARINGHOUSE

As your sales business grows, so do your responsibilities. More responsibilities mean more opportunities, though. With more opportunities, it can be easy to fall into the trap of working harder rather than working smarter.

We get caught up in the daily grind, processing orders, dealing with customer complaints, and attending endless meetings. Sometimes endless *meaningless* meetings. So how can you manage your time efficiently and effectively so you and your business can thrive?

First, you may have to remind yourself of your role. You're not here to process every internal process, create the product, or even solve every single problem that comes your way. Your primary job is to sell the *vision* and *value* of the product, get it to the right people, and then not get in their way.

You've got to be the clearinghouse.

What does that mean? Well, you need to either get the problem to the right person or get to the core of the problem yourself without getting stuck in the minutiae of meaningless details. Don't waste your time or your client's time.

Now, I know you're probably thinking: "Easier said than done, Mike!"

You're right!

It's incredibly easy to get bogged down in the details or feel like you're not doing enough to service your client the way they need. Before you know it, you're micromanaging everything happening within the business or in different silos of the company.

Remember my story from the last chapter about how the entire operations team wasn't too fond of my pushy attitude? It was all because I had waded knee-deep in the minutiae mud and didn't realize it. Thankfully, I had a manager pull me out of the muck and set me on the path again. Well, let this chapter act as a hazard warning: you're about to walk in a giant mud puddle if you think working harder is smarter. Working smarter will keep your feet out of the mud and allow you to continue moving your business forward.

Working smarter means making smart decisions about *what* you choose to work on. It means understanding your role and your value within the company. Knowing when to delegate tasks to others and when to focus on your own expertise. Being strategic and intentional with your time and energy, and not wasting it on tasks that don't bring value to the business. Don't waste time on activities which could be delegated to a data entry worker or technician. They're going to do a better job at it than you anyway.

Also, if gathering thousands of followers through posting content on LinkedIn fails to bring you any meaningful prospects, is it really worth your time? Of course not. But if every time you post, it generates interest from prospects, then keep at it! If you attend conferences and trade shows and walk away with no business cards or follow-up calls, is it worth your time? You can apply this way of thinking to any task you do.

It's so easy to end up giving your time to tasks that don't matter. It's a false sense of productivity. But the real gauge for productivity is whatever puts prospects into the pipeline.

And what about those pesky calls at 4:00 pm on a Friday? Well, not all calls are worth taking, but you won't know if you don't answer. The temptation to let them go to voicemail until Monday will be strong. But if you get in the habit of ignoring customers, you'll never retain them when you need to. If they perceive they are bothersome to you, then you've already lost. Your purpose as a sales professional is to be available to solve problems, to share your input, and to help your clients. You have to understand your *own* value and when to give it.

PRETENDING YOU HAVE ALL THE ANSWERS IS NOT ONLY DISHONEST, IT'S A RECIPE FOR BRINGING YOUR BUSINESS CRASHING DOWN.

Clients are always going to present problems—some simple, and some complex. But it's up to you to decide which problems to tackle and which ones to delegate. Get out your gauge and ask, "Am I the best person for this problem? Will I solve it fastest or would someone else handle it better than me?" A key point to remember is you won't always have all the answers. Never be afraid to share your expertise, but you cannot and should not tackle every issue on your own, especially the bigger your business gets. Pretending you have all the answers is not only dishonest, it's a recipe for bringing your business crashing down.

SHARE THE APPLAUSE

Oftentimes, young sales professionals who have become team leads see a simple problem as an opportunity to showcase their problem-solving skills. They are eager to rise up and shout to the world and their managers, "Look what I can do!"

Don't get me wrong, I love the eagerness to establish your value. But a word of caution: While it may seem admirable to bring attention to yourself, especially early on in your career, this kind of spotlight-seeking attitude can actually be detrimental to both the sales team and your business as a whole.

You need to recognize that not every problem requires your personal attention or insight. One of the most valuable skills a salesperson can learn early on is the ability to delegate tasks to the right people at the right time. This means finding opportunities for your support team to shine by passing the ball to someone standing closer to the net. Some of the best basketball players in the world are actually the best passers. Find an open teammate! But when passing the ball, don't always pass your support staff the toughest, soul-sucking problems. Instead, find ways to balance out the workload and responsibilities. Everyone needs a win, so set up easy wins to build confidence and establish positive momentum. That way, when the big problems arise, everyone is on their A+ game. Otherwise, you'll get an internal reputation as a "buck passer" or being lazy—and it will become more difficult to rally your support team members when you need them most.

When your team succeeds, make sure *everyone* is recognized for their contributions. Without recognition, people begin to feel like cogs in a machine. If you spotlight what everyone is doing well, it fosters a sense of camaraderie and unity, as well as a healthy competition among team members. A strong boost of morale and motivation within the team ensures everyone feels valued and appreciated. In the same way you seek to provide value to clients, seek to also provide value to those around you inside the organization. You won't speak to the client every day—but your team members are always around.

In order for your team to experience many wins, a lot of the responsibility falls on you as the leader. For some, when they get the big promotion or become a leader for the first time, they suddenly adopt an unapproachable demeanor or a "better than you" attitude.

But as a team leader, it's your responsibility to help others shine and grow in *their* roles. This means actively seeking out ways to mentor and support your team members, providing them with the necessary resources and guidance to succeed. By doing so, you'll build a team of confident, self-sufficient individuals who are able to tackle challenges head-on and deliver exceptional results.

IF YOU'RE GOOD AT GIVING *OTHERS* THE OPPORTUNITY TO SHINE, YOUR VALUE WILL BE RECOGNIZED BY CHIEF EXECUTIVES AND OTHER DECISION-MAKERS.

At the end of the day, for your business to succeed, you'll need a team succeeding *together*. No one person can do it all by themselves.

Maybe you feel like you've been passed up for a long time, watching others move ahead in their sales career while you're stuck in the same ol' grind. You might be thinking, "When is my moment coming, though?" Well, your moment is when you cash your check. Don't let the success of others deter or distract you from the success within your grasp.

However, if you're good at giving *others* the opportunity to shine, your value will be recognized by chief executives and other decision-makers. They'll see how unselfish you are, and you'll set yourself apart from the rest of the pack.

It's worth noting that not everyone is good at being unselfish. In today's world, people are often focused on themselves and their own success. Just look at the influencers on social media, only talking about their own alleged success, their carefree lifestyle, and then pitching products to their followers. This "influencer" mindset can be detrimental in a team environment. It says, "Your problem is you're not just like me." That's not being a problem solver—that's being a problem distributor.

If you can shift to being a problem solver, not a problem distributor, you'll avoid causing internal reputational damage. Instead, you'll be seen as a valuable asset to your team.

By embracing a collaborative mindset and actively seeking out opportunities to support and mentor your team, you can build a successful team dynamic. Remember to always share the applause, delegate tasks to the right people, and focus on the success of the team as a whole. By doing so, you'll be setting yourself and your team up for the long term.

BACK TO PERCEPTION

Here we are again, talking about the importance of perception and how it can affect your business as it grows. As you already know, perception is everything when it comes to building strong client relationships. You need to be able to see the world through *their* eyes and understand their needs to effectively deliver value. You see, it's not about chasing your own interests or taking the spotlight—it's about working with an unselfish mindset and putting the client first.

The best way to do this is by using your emotional intelligence (EQ) to your advantage. Emotional intelligence is a secret weapon that sets successful professionals apart from the rest of the pack. The ability to connect with clients on a deeper level, to understand their perspective, and to show them how they are truly heard and valued is what will raise your business to the next level.

Functioning and leading this way is like having a superpower that allows you to see the big picture at a 50,000 foot level. If you can zoom out and see everything from the client perspective, then you will naturally earn their trust and respect. If this doesn't come natural to you, then the key is to get really, really good at asking questions.

Why?

Because people *love* talking about themselves. People love sharing their insights, their views, their problems. If you open the door with questions and just let your prospect share, they will *give* you the 50,000 foot view! Often as salespeople, we have to fight the temptation to talk. Instead, we have to shift to asking questions. This in itself is emotional intelligence.

Let me tell you a story that perfectly illustrates the power of EQ. A client was upset, and my partner and I were summoned to their office for a meeting. My partner on the account was a seasoned pro in operations who had just transitioned into sales. As such, she was eager to dive into the details with her operations-minded brain. She even had a notebook full of all kinds of ideas to propose. She wanted to be prepared for anything and everything the client would bring up.

But here's the thing: You can't predict *anything*, especially when meeting with an upset client. I knew we needed to tread carefully and listen to the client before we could propose any solutions.

Fifteen minutes before the meeting, she asked me, "OK, Mike, what's our approach?" She was amped up, full of adrenaline—and probably caffeine.

I tried to calm her down and said, "Listen, we don't have an approach…."

The look of confusion washed over her face. "What do you mean? We need an approach here!" Her brain was still in operations mode, and in operations, if you don't have a plan, you are dead in the water.

"We don't know what *they* perceive as the problem yet," I continued, hoping she would understand what I was getting at.

She looked at me like I had switched languages on her. "I still don't understand, Mike," she replied.

"Well, shouldn't we wait to hear them out first before laying out a detailed outline?" I asked. "The issue may have nothing to do with all your notes."

Sure enough, after some probing with the client, we discovered the problem wasn't what either of us thought it was. Now my partner understood exactly what I meant.

SOMETIMES, THE BEST WAY TO SERVE A CLIENT IS TO TAKE A STEP BACK, *SHUT UP*, AND LISTEN.

Just because you have a million notes and ideas about a client's problem doesn't mean you are prepared. As my partner learned, you have to gain the perspective of the client first. We discovered the problem was a personality issue, a clash of styles that had spiraled out of control between our two companies. By exercising emotional intelligence and *listening* to the client, we were able to resolve the issue in one meeting, saving everyone time, effort, and stress. If we had gone in proposing a bunch of ideas in a notebook, we would only have made the problem worse.

Sometimes, the best way to serve a client is to take a step back, *shut up*, and listen. Remember, you have two ears and one mouth— use them accordingly. If you show up, guns blazing, you may inadvertently give the client more ammunition to use against you. Instead, it's better to approach the meeting with an open mind, free from any preconceived notions or hidden agendas. Listen to what they have to say and use your two ears and one mouth to your advantage.

To build lasting client relationships, you need to adopt a *relational* mindset. It's not just about getting the job done and closing a deal. Yes, completing the job professionally and efficiently is what you technically get paid for, but creating a connection, a rapport that transcends the transaction is *way* better. Always remember, when you walk into a meeting with a client, you're not just there to pitch a product—you're there to build trust.

Emotional intelligence, perception, and a relational mindset are the keys to successful client relationships and building your business. By mastering these skills, you can elevate your game and create a legacy that endures for years to come. So, go ahead—be bold, be creative, and be empathetic. Your clients will thank you for it!

ASSESSMENTS AND COMMUNICATION

We have talked a lot about the best methods to use in sales and finding what works best for you. Understanding who you are and the people you work with is vital to a growing business. You don't want to be a distant stranger to your coworkers or to your clients. You definitely don't want to be guessing what makes your customer tick five meetings into discussing a deal. If you hope to achieve meaningful growth and progress, you must take the time to truly connect with those around you.

So what can you do?

Well, one tool to use is a personality test. There are many available, but I found this to be very insightful and beneficial to understand how I myself tick. The more you know about yourself, the more confident you can become in understanding how to relate to others.

After all, if you don't know who *you* are, how do you expect to ever truly understand others?

Whatever personality test you end up taking, it's more than just assigning yourself a number or letter. It's about finding out the other personality types, too. After all, you're not going to be able to go into a first meeting with a prospect and say, "Hello there, could you take this personality test before we proceed?" That's a sure way to end a conversation before it begins.

I'm a firm believer you should choose your own assessment. But to help you know where to start, here's a short list of some of the most popular presented in alphabetical order to keep it free of my own personal bias:

- Birkman Method
- DISC Assessment
- Enneagram
- Eysenck Personality Inventory
- HEXACO
- HIGH5 Test
- Hogan Assessments (Multiple versions)
- Keirsey Temperament Sorter (aligns with Myers–Briggs)
- Myers–Briggs Type Indicator (MBTI)

There are plenty of others, of course, so do your research and find the one that fits you best. Maybe do several to get a better grasp on yourself. But don't just do it for yourself! Make sure you read up on the other types the assessment covers. Learn to recognize their traits in the people you interact with. This gives you a bit of a "cheat sheet" for knowing how to communicate with others so you can make an essential positive first impression and establish trust right out the gate.

For instance, engineers are highly intellectual and prefer to talk about the quality of the features. They are very data-driven, rather than feelings-motivated, and often tend to be Type A personalities like myself. Type A engineers will analyze an issue, whereas Type B individuals will just go out and take action based on what they feel is best. When I'm interacting with an engineer type, it's my job to reciprocate, to focus my Type A tendencies on the operational details. If I'm dealing with a more emotional, Type B, spiritual person, though, I've got to bend myself to discuss how the product will make them *feel* or how it will benefit them on a personal level.

Suppose you're dealing with a quick decision-maker. In that case, you can't muddy it up with too much information and chitchat. You've got to know how to get straight to the point to match them. Being aware of these personality differences is key to effective communication.

Remember, the burden of communication is on the *sender* to make their message clear. The receiver's job is to ask for clarification if they don't understand. It's essential to uncover meaning without conflict so you can resolve any issues that may arise.

I once worked on a project where my partner admitted to being confused about what the client

IF YOU ASSUME, YOU ARE DOOMED.

was asking. I said, "Well, then *ask* for them to clarify before you move into action."

If you assume, you are doomed.

Sure, that sounds a bit cheesy, but it can help you remember to never assume. You are better off going to the casino and putting money into a slot machine than assuming you understand a client's problem. Simply asking for clarity can save you a *lot* of time and prevent misunderstandings. It's amazing the difference one question can make.

Knowing your communication style and personality type while being aware of others can help you navigate different situations with more confidence. Your business is nothing without people, so you might as well get to know them, right? Sales is not a product business. It's a *people* business. But it's also a business where you need to understand what works best for *you* in order to find lasting success.

By investing in yourself, you also invest in those around you, building a business rooted in strong, meaningful connections. Ultimately, if you build your business the right way, the smart way, the Sales Hunter way, you will reap the rewards.

CONCLUSION

You may have noticed throughout this book I like to keep things pretty simple. The thing about common sense in sales is how surprisingly uncommon it's become. There is more noise than ever before. One of my goals here has been to cut through the noise and restore some dignity and decency to the sales profession.

So if at any point in this book, you said to yourself, "Huh, this makes sense. This should've been obvious. Why didn't I think of this before?," then I hope it won't end there for you. I hope you'll actually take the step to incorporate these lessons into your sales strategy.

Furthermore, if you've learned even one lesson from me, not only do I hope it will change the trajectory of *your* sales career, but I hope you'll be willing to share it with others. The whole reason I sat down to write this book was because I didn't want to hoard everything I've learned in my three decades of experience. Just like how my father's friends taught me how to hunt all those years ago in my childhood, I now want to pass on everything I've learned. So if you enjoyed this book, I hope you'll refer it to others.

ONE OF MY GOALS HERE HAS BEEN TO CUT THROUGH THE NOISE AND RESTORE SOME DIGNITY AND DECENCY TO THE SALES PROFESSION.

In the end, I hope the lessons here have given you a renewed drive and fresh perspective to hunt your next big deal. If you feel too far gone, like it's too late for you to turn the ship around, I promise you it's not. I've purposefully worked to share insights here that you can apply immediately. If you take one idea you've learned in this book and apply it today, you'll already be a better Sales Hunter than you were yesterday. You'll be one step closer to turning over the rock hiding treasure.

I'm not perfect by any means. By sharing stories from my own experiences, I wanted to show I've made mistakes—plenty of them—and learned from them. You can too. There are no truly lost opportunities if you have learned from failure. You can always get back up, shake yourself off, and try again.

Also, I would be remiss if I didn't take a moment to thank you for taking the time to read this. Out of all the sales books out there, all the articles, all the online gurus, you picked up this book and gave me the most precious thing you possess—your time. I truly appreciate it and hope it's been worthy of your time. If so, I'd be grateful for a review on Amazon or Goodreads so we can help spread the word to more salespeople.

And finally, if you want to continue this conversation about Sales Hunting and continue to improve, I'd love to chat with you. Whether you are a young sales professional, a sales manager, or a seasoned sales veteran like myself, there's a lot we can learn from one another. I started up my sales consulting business JBI (Just Buy In) for this very reason—to help other sales professionals find success in their careers the way I have. My driving purpose with JBI is to encourage people to come talk to me more because sales is really about having a discussion. My hope in this book is to kick off the discussion, whether that's between you and your supervisor, your team members, or you and I connecting. You can learn more at our website:

Sales can feel like a lonely profession, but it doesn't have to be. So whether you connect with us at JBI or not, it's important you continue to connect with others for support. Otherwise when you start to burn out, you won't have anyone around to help you put out the flames. Just keep in mind there's a difference between receiving supportive counsel and just sitting around to complain.

At the end of the day, the keys to success are in your hand. Not every door will open for you, but your set of keys will open up the *right* doors for you if you persevere and always keep moving. The treasure is out there to find. So let's go hunting.

CONTACT

Michael Hinkle
info@michaelhinkle.com
LinkedIn: https://www.linkedin.com/in/michaeldhinkle/
JBI – Just Buy In: https://www.linkedin.com/company/justbuyin/

JBI Consulting Services is a carefully created one-on-one coaching experience to help you take the various topics discussed in this book and apply them to your own Sales Career. While some coaches focus on one-size-fits-most, JBI takes your own unique gifts into account and we develop strong relationship-building skills based on your strengths in your market niche. You are as unique as an individual, so why would you seek out solutions to improve your business that are not also as unique as you? Just like in this book, we develop your coaching experience around you, the client.

JBI also offers motivational speaker programs centered around the different chapters in this book. We can also offer an overall presentation of the core principles of this book to enable your Sales Force to create more successful tactics. We are convinced through years of implementation that these tactics will drive more business through your doors. The moment one stops learning and improving their sales skills is the moment when the competition gains a competitive advantage.

ABOUT THE AUTHOR

As the oldest of four children, I've always led a very independent life. When I was a teenager, I was in the Boy Scouts and was told that I would never become an Eagle Scout due to the fact I was not a strong swimmer. So I became a competitive swimmer and swam through my college years. Oh, I earned my Eagle Scout badge as well.

When I graduated from college, I noticed a game being played in a local park called "rugby." I started looking into this game and was told I was too short to play. So obviously, I played the game for the next six years at a competitive level.

As you can see, every time in my life someone told me what I could *not* do, I responded by saying, "Watch me." This is the approach I have taken my entire life. I have always had a deep desire to do what no one expects of me simply because I place no limitations on myself.

Both of my parents had careers that were very demanding. My mother was an Emergency Room RN and my father worked for the Sheriff's Department. Life had no gray areas for me. As the great quote from *Star Wars* goes, "Do or do not. There is no try." Simple as that.

Just twenty-four hours out of high school on my first shift as a lifeguard, I was presented with a life-changing opportunity when I had to rescue a young girl from drowning. After performing CPR, she began breathing again and left my care for the hospital alive and well. While most might revel in this success, my parents led me to reflect on the lessons I could learn from the event. How could I prevent this from happening again on my watch in the future? This is a focus that remains with me to this very day. Wins are great, but what did we learn from it?

One might think that through these events and my own drive to succeed I might just be wrapped a little tight. However, it's not the case. What I learned from all this is that the formula for success is elementary. That success in life stems from simply applying basic and well-proven skill sets in a consistent manner, ensuring the steps you take lead you to the objective of being the best person you can be. It is not hard, but it does take total commitment and a deep desire to always come out on top.

I hope you enjoyed this book as I detail the wins and setbacks my career has put me through and the rewards achieved by keeping to the basics. I'm a strong believer that the biggest impediment to leading a successful life does not come between your ears but is the result of a heart that drives you on no matter what the situation is. The darkest clouds always seem to result in the brightest sunrises. Good luck to you with your treasure hunt.

Printed in the USA
CPSIA information can be obtained
at www.ICGtesting.com
JSHW022315291223
54568JS00002B/17